More Quick Watercolor Quilts

DINA PAPPAS

Martingale™
& COMPANY

CREDITS

President • Nancy J. Martin
CEO • Daniel J. Martin
Publisher • Jane Hamada
Editorial Director • Mary V. Green
Editorial Project Manager • Tina Cook
Technical Editor • Dawn Anderson
Copy Editor • Pamela Mostek
Design and Production Manager • Stan Green
Illustrator • Laurel Strand
Cover and Text Designer • Trina Stahl
Photographer • Brent Kane

That Patchwork Place® is an
imprint of Martingale & Company™.

More Quick Watercolor Quilts
© 2001 by Dina Pappas

Martingale & Company
20205 144th Avenue NE
Woodinville, WA 98072-8478 USA
www.martingale-pub.com

Printed in China
06 05 04 03 02 01   8 7 6 5 4 3 2 1

MISSION STATEMENT

We are dedicated to providing quality products
and service by working together to inspire creativity
and to enrich the lives we touch.

Library of Congress Cataloging-in-Publication Data

Pappas, Dina.
   More quick watercolor quilts / Dina Pappas.
      p. cm.
   ISBN 1-56477-364-7
      1. Patchwork—Patterns. 2. Patchwork quilts. 3. Fusible
   materials in sewing. 4. Watercolor quilting. I. Title.

TT835 .P356 2001
746.46'041—dc21   2001022254

DEDICATION

To my stepfather, Bill Nerud, for his unwavering support and faith
that there would be more than one book.

ACKNOWLEDGMENTS

Thanks to the following people:

To my stepfather, Bill Nerud, for opening your doors during our move and letting me take over your dining room to quilt. I enjoyed our talks and being able to share my designing ideas.

To Karen Tomczak for the power lunches and brainstorming.

To Marguerite McManus for your beautiful machine quilting on "Garland Irish Chain," "Blooming Hedges with Swags," and "Lacy Eight-Pointed Star of Poinsettias," and for your feedback and support.

To Sue Bergerson for your generous support in creating a great quilting haven. Also, to the staff at Quilt Works in Anchorage for your support, enthusiasm, and for doting on my children. The snacks and buttons let me stock up on supplies while the boys were entertained.

To Kathy Seals for your technical assistance in triangle piecing.

To my students for your willingness to learn with me and for all you taught me about combining fabrics to make it work. Your feedback gives me direction, lets me know what else to say, and a chance to say it.

To my husband, Jim, for encouraging me—thanks for the support to upgrade the sewing room. Also, thanks to my sons, Jack and Charley, for telling me my quilts are pretty and letting me use the computer.

To Freudenburg Nonwovens, Pellon Consumer Products Division, Tina Schwager, and Charles Arana for making and supplying the interfacing I requested. With the right tools, the door is wide open to create beautiful quilts.

To the people at Martingale & Company for their excellent work in promoting my quilting. You do a magical job with the cardboard boxes of stuff I send you and turn it into a beautiful, well-marketed book. Thank you for your faith in me, your enthusiasm, and hard work.

Diamond Jubilee by Dina Pappas, 2000, Tecumseh, Michigan, 74" x 89".
A center diamond framed by a shaped border gives an elegant look to this quilt, which is suitable for a gift and sure to be an heirloom. The finished Diamond Jubilee block measures 27½" x 35". The quilt was made using 3" squares.

Contents

Preface

Cooking up these quilts grew from taking a traditional quilt and applying my watercolor method of selecting fabric and piecing with interfacing. The traditional pattern, Trip Around the World, adapts perfectly to using interfacing piecing. When I used my watercolor method of fabric selection, I loved the results. Classes based on that quilt further excited me with the layout options and beauty of the quilts students were making. The "Blooming Hedges" quilts on pages 15 and 29 came from listening to students' feedback regarding the use of fewer fabrics. I also explored the setting options and tried both appliqué embellishments and watercolor swags in different quilts. I wondered what else could be done with this fabric combination and piecing technique. I tried designing a Double Irish Chain quilt using watercolor fabrics and loved the garlands created. Then I played with the Double Irish Chain layout, carrying a variation of the block design into the border and adding appliqué to create "Celtic Garden Maze," shown on page 65.

Because these quilts can be designed and stitched so quickly, there are many large projects in the book. Many of the designs are made from repeated panels. "Garden Sampler" on page 51 is made from a fun set of designs that can be used to create a whole quilt, used as a block-of-the month, or used individually for small gifts. Traditional quilting designs are transformed with the beauty of watercolor and the ease of interfacing piecing.

Lacy Eight-Pointed Star of Poinsettias by Dina Pappas, 2000, Colbert, Washington, 81" x 81"; quilted by Marguerite McManus. The poinsettias in the fabric were used to paint holes in the star design. The quilt was made using 3" squares.

Blooming Hedges with Swags by Dina Pappas, 2000, Colbert, Washington, 86½" x 86½"; quilted by Marguerite McManus. Swags in the open areas add flowers without the work of appliqué. The quilt was made with 3" squares.

Introduction

I'M VERY HAPPY to continue exploring watercolor possibilities in this sequel to my book, *Quick Watercolor Quilts*. I discovered a secret when experimenting with piecing different shapes on fusible interfacing. The angles of the intersecting seams had to be equal. The technique applied easily to designs with squares that were all the same size. Other options also worked. A combination of squares and rectangles worked. A fun surprise: 60-degree equilateral triangles worked. The book introduces these new shapes to fusible interfacing piecing.

Just a few fabrics, some fusible interfacing, and a little time are the ingredients needed for the projects in this book. Many people appreciate quilting but don't have the time or skills to sew all those pieces together accurately. When they see the technique with fusible interfacing they get excited. The results are so simple and accurate. Best of all, the patterns emerge quickly. Repeated panels, blocks, and different pieced shapes quickly combine into beautiful projects even a beginner can complete.

"What is watercolor quilting?" my dad asked me. I explained that watercolor quilting is a technique in which the pattern of the quilt emerges from the fabrics blending together. My watercolor method requires as few as two or three fabrics. The key is to begin with a floral print that shows large areas of background. Combining the floral with another fabric that imitates the background of the first allows the fabrics to seemingly melt together when they are pieced. My method is a combination of watercolor techniques and traditional high-contrast piecing, and it results in a blended shape that floats on a contrasting background.

People often comment that I must have lots of patience to put together all those pieces. I don't. I want those pieces sewn together as quickly as possible before I run out of quilting time. I solve the piecing problem with fusible interfacing. The interfacing foundation secures the design, reduces the number of seams required, and increases accuracy.

I have presented just a taste of the possibilities. My goal is to expand the uses for the fusible interfacing technique and give you another look at using watercolor fabrics.

Small Garden Sampler by Dina Pappas, 2000, Tecumseh, Michigan, 39½" x 39½". Four blocks are framed by a checkerboard, then bordered by a fun garden-theme fabric. Combine your favorite blocks from "Garden Sampler" on page 51 to make a similar wall hanging or simply make one block for a quick gift. The finished panel for "Small Garden Sampler" measures 31½" x 31½". The quilt was made using 2" squares.

Supplies

Fabrics

I PREFER to use 100 percent–cotton fabrics for quiltmaking, but since the interfacing foundation stabilizes your watercolor quilt, you can use other fabrics normally considered too bulky or fragile for quilts. Even silks and decorator fabrics can be used with this technique. See "Fabric Selection" on pages 11–14 for an in-depth discussion of fabric options.

The yardage requirements for quilts in this book are based on 42" of usable width after prewashing. If your fabric is narrower than 42", you may need additional yardage.

Interfacing

IT IS important for the watercolor pieces to be fused securely to the interfacing grid; however, you also want to add as little bulk as possible. Use lightweight fusible interfacing for cotton. For heavier fabrics, use medium-weight fusible interfacing.

Interfacings are available in a variety of widths, including 22", 44", or 48" wide. Often the width varies along the length of the piece. If the interfacing along an edge doesn't extend under the full width of the pieces, don't worry. There will be enough interfacing to anchor the pieces and provide a foundation for flipping and sewing.

Printed grids are available on some interfacings. Printed grid sizes come in 1", 1½", and 2" squares. See "Piecing with Interfacing" on page 24 for how to use grid sizes different from your planned piece size or shape. Whatever the grid, make sure your interfacing is fusible. There are some products with a grid that are not. Check with your fingers for the bumpy dots; they are what secure the fabric.

Batting

WHEN USING an interfacing grid, choose a thin, low-loft batting to make quilting easier. With thinner battings there is less bulk to fit under the machine.

Thread

WHEN PIECING and machine quilting, use 100 percent–cotton thread. Cotton thread breaks infrequently, allowing you to maintain your rhythm while machine quilting. For machine appliqué, use transparent (monofilament) thread for the top thread. Choose a cotton thread for the bobbin with a color matching the piece being appliquéd.

Rotary Cutter and Mat

FOR FAST, accurate cutting, I prefer to use a rotary cutter. Keep fresh blades on hand and change them often. I frequently use my cutting mat as my design area. I like a large size, 23" x 35", to give me room to square panels. An 18" x 24" mat accommodates the width of the fusible interfacing as you prepare grids.

Rulers

USE A clear acrylic ruler to guide the rotary blade when cutting. Choose a 24" ruler for general strip cutting and squaring tops. A 6" square ruler is nice for cutting single strips. Rulers with 45-degree lines on them are nice when mitering borders. To cut triangles, such as those used in the "Four Vintage Baskets" quilt on page 72, you will need a ruler with 60-degree angle lines or a special triangle ruler.

Worktable

A PERFECT cutting surface for your mat is one that is approximately 4" lower than your elbow, about the height of kitchen countertops. This gives you cutting leverage without back strain. A dedicated work space is nice but optional.

Scissors

YOU WILL need a sewing shears for trimming excess batting. A small scissors is great for snipping threads.

Planning Tools

GRAPH PAPER works well for planning your design and creating original patterns. You'll then have a design sheet for reference should you decide to make the quilt again. It is helpful to record information on the sheet, such as yardage requirements, number and width of strips to cut, and any special construction techniques needed. You'll also need pencils, erasers, and a ruler. You may also want a calculator for figuring yardage requirements, finished sizes, and the number of strips to cut.

Marking Tools

USE A water-soluble marker or a No. 2 pencil to mark triangle sewing dots or to make grids if you're not using a preprinted interfacing. Be aware that if your pencil is too sharp, it will tear the interfacing.

Use chalk to mark the quilt design if you plan to machine quilt. For hand quilting, use a pencil or water-soluble marker for a longer-lasting line.

Reducing Glass

TO HELP view a design from a distance in a closed-in area, you can use a reducing glass. It works like a magnifying glass, but it shrinks an image rather than enlarges it. Looking at a design through a reducing glass or from a distance gives a new perspective and helps identify problem areas. You can get the same results by looking through the wrong end of binoculars or the viewfinder of a camera. You can also purchase a peephole, like those used in the front door, at a building-supply store. All allow you to step back even if your room is small.

Window Template

USE A cardboard window template to help visualize the amount of pattern that will be visible in your finished square or triangle. Cut the cardboard to the size of your cut square or triangle and cut a hole from the center the size of the finished square or triangle, leaving a ¼" frame all around (see photo). This ¼" frame covers the seam allowances that disappear when pieces are joined.

Use a window template to preview the finished square or triangle.

Lighting

IN ORDER to determine if your selected fabrics blend well, make sure your work area has good lighting. It is preferable to check your fabric selections in natural light before you purchase them. Hold the fabrics up to a window if possible.

Iron

AN IRON is essential for piecing with fusible interfacing. Keep one near your sewing machine and worktable for fusing pieces to your grid and for pressing seams. Fusible interfacing can leave residue on your iron so be careful to keep the iron on the fabric and off the interfacing as you press. Keep the soleplate clean. If residue gets on your iron, it can be easily transferred to your fabric and can be difficult to remove. Clean your iron as necessary with an iron cleaner. After the seams are sewn, use a press cloth on the front to avoid marks at the seam intersections.

Pressing Surface

RAISE YOUR ironing board to the height of your worktable, if possible, and butt the two together. Your design space will be increased, and you'll be able to slide your work onto the ironing board without disturbing the layout. Portable pressing mats with cutting mats on the reverse side are also great for working on the floor or in front of the television.

Sewing Machine

MOST STRAIGHT-STITCH sewing machines work well for the projects in this book. For machine quilting, a few additional features are desirable. For free-motion quilting, you need to be able to move the quilt sandwich freely with the presser foot down. Some machines have buttons that drop or disengage the feed dogs—the teeth under the presser foot that push the fabric through the machine. Others have a button on the top or dial on the side that reduces the amount of pressure on the presser foot to zero. Take out your sewing machine's instruction manual to review, follow the manufacturer's instructions, and set the machine to the darning setting.

Having the right presser foot can make your sewing experience more enjoyable. If the following feet didn't come with your sewing machine, look for them at a quilt shop or sewing machine service center.

Walking foot with guide bar: This attachment feeds multiple layers of fabric through the machine at the same rate, helping to prevent puckering. Also called an even-feed foot, it "walks" over the top layer of fabric as the feed dogs pull the bottom layer along. It is used for straight-line quilting. A guide bar that screws into the walking foot allows you to stitch a parallel line of quilting without marking the quilt top.

Free-motion quilting foot, also called a darning foot: These are often round, clear plastic feet used for stipple quilting. Some free-motion feet have a spring action that holds the fabric down as the stitch is made, then releases, allowing you to move the quilt.

Quilting Gloves or Rubber Finger Tips

QUILTING GLOVES with little gripper dots on the palm side allow you to grip interfacing panels and control the quilt sandwich with less pressure from your hands. They're especially nice when you're machine quilting a large project because they lessen the stress on your back and neck.

Hand quilters might want to try rubber fingertips, available at office-supply stores. They make it easier to pull hand-quilting needles (Betweens) through a quilt sandwich. Quilters can also place them on the first three fingers and thumb of each hand to get a better grip on a quilt when machine quilting.

Fabric Selection

THERE ARE THREE types of fabrics required for quick watercolor quilts. The success of your project depends on finding the following:

1. An "edge" fabric—one with a widely spaced floral print

2. A "background" fabric—one that matches the background color in your edge fabric

3. A "full floral" fabric—one with a dense floral print that works with your edge and background fabrics

This section describes the fabric selection process in detail, complete with example photos to keep you on track. You'll learn to look at fabrics differently and you'll find terrific uses for prints you might otherwise have passed by.

Most projects require five fabrics or less to keep it simple, but feel free to add more fabrics if you want. You can start by sticking to the formula and then experiment by combining more fabrics to create more complex watercolor designs.

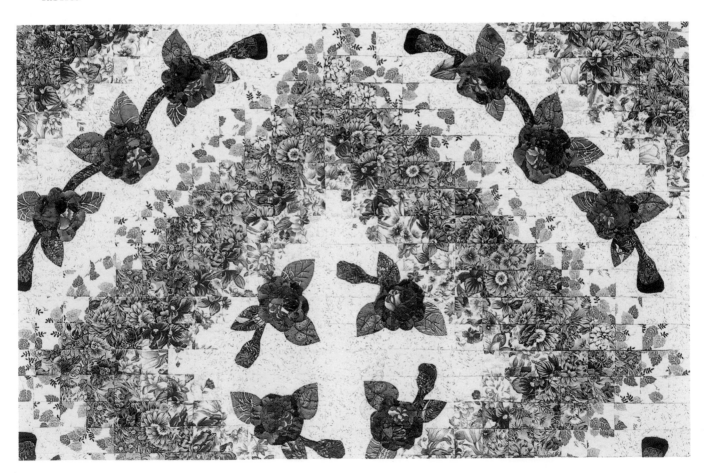

Combining Three Fabrics

STUNNING WATERCOLOR quilts can be made with just three fabrics. I used three fabrics for "Twined Vines Runner and Place Mats" on page 41, the "Lacy Eight-Pointed Star of Poinsettias" on page 6, and "Garden Sampler" on page 51. "Garden Sampler" calls for additional fabrics to make the garden motifs, but the bouquets are created using the three-fabric formula.

Edge Fabrics

I've found that it's best to begin with the edge fabric. When selecting fabric, you may be tempted to start with the floral focus of your quilt, but if you can't find companion edge and background fabrics, you will be disappointed.

Edge fabrics form the bridge between the background and floral areas, and they are often hard to recognize in the finished quilt. A good edge fabric is the key to success. When I find one I like, I stock up.

The best edge fabrics have widely spaced, medium- to large-scale floral patterns with strong contrast between the floral motifs and the background. When these requirements are met, the fabric can be rotary cut into squares without worrying about "fussy" cutting. Avoid prints with flowers that blend into the background since they don't provide a crisp, defining edge.

The floral motif of a successful edge fabric will fill only part of your piece. For example, a 1" flower would fill a corner or side of a 2" square, so look for large and medium flowers and skip over the small-scale prints. Also, keep your piece size in mind. A floral motif suitable for 2" squares may be too small for 3" squares.

Good edge fabrics: The backgrounds of these prints contrast strongly with the floral motifs.

Poor edge fabrics (left to right): The flowers are too small, not enough background shows, the floral design melts into the background.

Different-sized pieces and print scales

Background Fabrics

A good background fabric is one that repeats the background color and texture of your edge fabric. If you find a fabric that is almost what you're looking for, but not quite, try turning it over. The back side may be the perfect match.

To test a background, overlap it with your edge fabric and step back. If you notice just the floral print, you've done well. If the background stands out clearly, try again. Compare your fabrics in good lighting when making your selections—try carrying your fabrics to a window to view them in natural light.

White and cream backgrounds are easier to match than colored backgrounds. If you can't find a good match, select another edge fabric.

Full-Floral Fabrics

Finally, look for a dense floral print to complete the fabric requirements. I usually hold up the bolt of edge fabric and compare it with bolts of densely covered floral fabrics on the shelf. When I find a print with similar tones, I compare it more carefully, checking to see if the foliage designs work well together. My goal is to match the colors and styles of the flowers. Light, airy, edge fabric blends best with a similarly delicate floral. Edge fabrics with stronger floral elements demand bold floral companions; however, mixed styles can work. A few light areas in the full floral print can help blend the fabrics.

Again, test the blending of the fabrics by layering them and stepping back. Can you create a whole flower from the pieces of each fabric? If you can see an obvious line between the fabrics, they may not work well together.

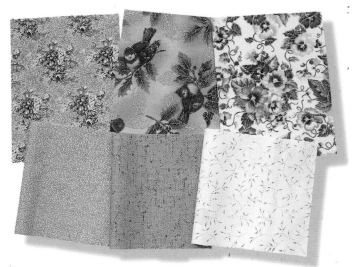

Good edge and background matches; the background fabrics match the background texture and color of the edge fabrics.

The background fabric's texture and color do not match the edge fabric.

The background closely matches the edge fabric, producing a smooth watercolor blend between pieces.

It is important for the full-floral fabric to blend with the edge fabric, but you also want it to contrast with the background fabric. If any blossoms in the full-floral print are the same color as the background fabric, "holes" will appear in your watercolor design. Selective cutting can remove areas that contain undesired colors.

Combination Prints

Combination prints can simplify the fabric selection and cutting processes. These fabrics work as "two-for-ones" because they yield both edge and full-floral squares. I used combination fabrics for "Lacy Eight-Pointed Star Wall Hanging" (page 46) and "Small Garden Sampler" (page 7).

Look for prints of large bouquets that show wide gaps of background. You need suitable edge fabric around the border of each bouquet and full-floral fabric in the middle. Just add a matching background and you have a watercolor combination.

Decorator prints often have patterns that are easily cut into both edge and full-floral pieces. They also have large-scale motifs suitable for large pieces. Try the decorator section for a change of pace and inspiration. If you have leftover scraps from making drapes or a slipcover, you might want to make coordinating bedding.

Using More than Three Fabrics

ADDING EXTRA floral fabrics provides a bridge to better blend a watercolor combination and gives more depth to the quilt. Four fabrics blend to create "Diamond Jubilee" (page 4), "Blooming Hedges with Swags" (page 15), and "Blooming Hedges" (page 29). The fabrics blend to create a swag of flowers floating on the background. By adding another fabric in the center of the swag, you can make it bolder. Or have one side of the swag be different than the other as in "Two-Color Blooming Hedges" (page 34). To choose

additional fabrics, check to see that each fabric bridges the colors between the fabrics on either side of it. The flowers should gradually get denser and larger in scale when moving from the background to full-floral.

Good combinations of full-floral, edge, and background fabrics

Large bouquet prints that yield both edge and full-floral squares

Adding additional fabrics

Blooming Hedges with Swags by Dina Pappas, 2000, Colbert, Washington, 86½" x 86½"; quilted by Marguerite McManus. Swags in the open areas add flowers without the work of appliqué. The quilt was made with 3" squares and four different fabrics.

Designing Quilts

When I make a watercolor quilt, I aim for a broderie perse effect, the appearance that the watercolor shape was cut out whole and appliquéd to the background. Creating an illusion is the goal of watercolor quiltmaking; you want to disguise the fact the quilt is made of simple pieces.

Graphing Designs

I usually start the design process by sketching a basic shape on graph paper. Then when I have a pleasing design, I treat each square on the graph paper as a square of fabric.

The quilt plans in this book include master design grids for you to follow; however, graph paper allows you to try your hand at an original pattern. Use your grid as a handy reference tool. It is the perfect place to keep notes on yardage, assembly, and quilting.

Designing Shapes

My students often comment that designing a watercolor quilt is just like putting together a puzzle. You evaluate each piece, looking for the perfect spot for it on the grid. I enjoy the mystery involved because I still never know how a quilt will look until it is finished.

I lay out the plain background pieces first, move to the edges of the watercolor design, then fill in the middle with full-floral pieces.

Reading the Edge Fabric

To create a strong outline, find the most dominate leaf or flower in your edge piece. Stand back and look at your fabric to see which color stands out. This will be your "paintbrush color." Notice which part of the piece is filled with the dominant foliage or flower. Also note which section of the piece has background pockets. Now, position these pieces to form shapes.

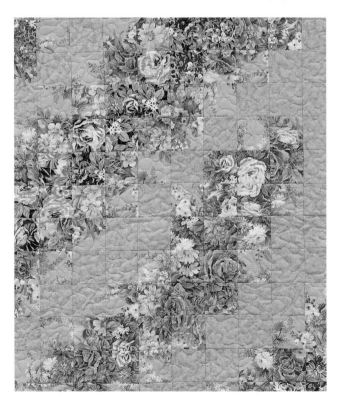

Reading the edge fabric: The light blue sections of "Blooming Hedges with Swags" soften the edges.

Placing Edge Pieces

SUCCESSFUL EDGE fabrics eliminate the need for fancy cutting. Simply use your rotary cutter to cut fabric strips into pieces. Placing edge pieces is usually a challenge for my students. Relax and don't fuss. Pick up the stack of edge pieces, take the top piece, and loosely interpret what you see. Decide where best to put it and quickly move to the next. You can fine-tune the shape later, switching pieces if you don't like the way it looks.

Basic Edge Shapes

Large Diagonal

For squares, these pieces look like half-square triangles because the pattern divides the square in half diagonally. Half the square shows foliage, and the other half shows background. On a triangle, the pattern also divides the triangle in half, giving a diagonal slant to the foliage.

Large Diagonals

Small Diagonal

Like large diagonals, these pieces show foliage in one corner only, but the proportions are different. A "small" diagonal shows just a tiny bit of floral; the rest of the piece is background. Small diagonals are great for building smooth curves. If you choose an edge fabric that doesn't have large background areas, you won't find many small diagonals among your pieces.

Small Diagonals

Full Edge

These pieces are nearly filled with flowers, leaving background showing on one edge only. Full edge pieces add fullness and height to curves. Use a window template to make sure a line of background will remain after the piece is sewn. If the seam allowance would completely eliminate the background, save the piece for filling full-floral areas.

Full Edges

Half Edge

A straight line appears to cut these pieces in half. Less than half of the piece shows foliage and the remaining half shows background. Use these squares to build inner curves, or combine them to make rounded edges.

Valley

Three sides of the piece have foliage, while the fourth side has a V-shaped pocket of background cut into it. Use valley pieces to join two curves, giving your design a scalloped edge.

Tip

Look for a single bloom nestled within a V-shaped area of background. Use tip pieces to make the point of a border block or to end a spray of blooms.

Edge-Shape Combinations

It's easy to make curves and build sprays of flowers when you know what kind of pieces to use. To build smooth curves, make sure the foliage on each piece forms an even bridge between its neighboring pieces. Count the number of pieces needed to complete the curve. To create an outer curve, use your fullest foliage piece at the center and gradually decrease the amount of foliage as you move toward the outer edges. To create an inner curve, use a small amount of foliage at the center and gradually increase the foliage as you move to the outer edges.

You'll want to use certain types of squares to create particular shapes. The combinations found on page 19 are used in this book.

Half Edges

Valleys

Tips

Three-Square Outer Curve

Build rounded edges with three squares—a diagonal square at each end and one full edge piece in the middle.

Five-Square Outer Curve

Build outer curves with five squares—a small diagonal at each end, half edges in the second and fourth squares, and a full edge in the middle.

Three-Square Inside Curve

Build inner curves with four squares—in the center, place two squares that are about one-third filled with foliage and a diagonal square on each side.

Placing Full-Floral Squares

ONCE THE edges are formed, fill in the centerpieces with full-florals to complete the design. As you position these pieces, try to blend and strengthen the edge and build complete flowers. Blending prevents a "cross-stitch" look of abrupt edges.

Take advantage of the different flower colors in your full-floral pieces. Look at your fabric and locate the flowers that best echo the background fabric. If you have a beige background, find a light colored flower. Place these light squares near the edges to soften them and blend them into the background. See the "Full-Floral Squares" photo on page 20 for a detail from "Two-Color Blooming Hedges."

Building blooms with the help of edge squares adds a realistic look to a bouquet. Shift edge pieces as needed to form flowers. Try rotating pieces to correct chopped petals. When a piece has one flower on it, surround it with pieces that have small bits of the same flower color to complete the bloom. See the "Building Blooms" photo on page 20 for a detail from "Garden Sampler."

Three-Square Outer Curve: Detail of
"Lacy Eight-Pointed Star Wall Hanging"

Five-Square Outer Curve: Detail of "Twisted Vines Runner"

Four-Square Inside Curve: Detail of
"Lacy Eight-Pointed Star Wall Hanging"

Full-Floral Squares: Detail of "Two-Color Blooming Hedges"

Evaluating the Design

ONCE YOU'VE filled all the squares on your grid, step back to get a fresh look at the design. I often drag students away at this point because this is important. Go get a cup of coffee or take a break. Then, look at the piece from across the room. If your work space is small, use a reducing glass to see how the quilt will look from a distance. See what works and pinpoint areas that bother you. Check for completed flowers. Strengthen your shape by filling in holes, softening curves, and blending edges.

Selective cutting along a strip can find pieces to fill any "holes." If the full-floral squares have too many open areas, the design may not fill in. Now it is easier to see what piece is missing. Sometimes cutting a few more squares to play with makes a big difference.

This is the stage where I sometimes notice that the background is not a good match. It may be too white or not yellow enough. Maybe the edge and full-floral weren't made for each other. It is better to change fabrics than to finish something that doesn't work. The pieces removed can be saved for another project—it never hurts to have a stash of squares when you're making watercolor quilts. Position a few new background pieces and check to see whether they blend better before you replace the whole fabric.

Make your repairs and turn on the iron. You could fuss forever, but at some point just stop and fuse the design.

Building Blooms—surrounding a single colored square to complete the flower: Detail of "Garden Sampler"

Selectively cutting squares

Piecing with Interfacing

A T FIRST GLANCE you might look at one of my quilts and wonder who would want to sew together that many pieces? I often see that look on people's faces. The fusible-piecing technique reduces the number of seams needed to join the top, increases accuracy, and anchors the design you worked so hard to create. When quilters see how few seams are necessary to join a fused watercolor design, they understand why others find the technique so appealing.

Which designs can be pieced with interfacing? Any design that can be sewn straight through from one side to the other. If you can fold and stitch all rows in one direction, then clip and stitch rows in the remaining direction and create angles of equal size where seams intersect, you can use an interfacing grid for the base. Even equilateral triangle shapes work because you can stitch three sets of seams from one side of the interfacing grid to the other, and angles of equal size are created where the seams intersect. This technique will not work for diamonds since the angles formed at the seam intersections are not equal.

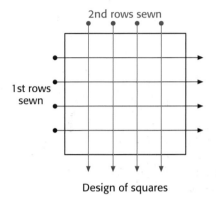

Design of squares

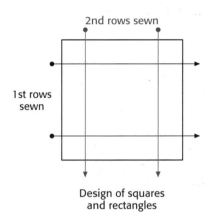

Design of squares
and rectangles

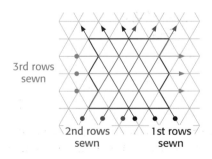

Design of equilateral
triangles

For ease in stitching, you can also combine blocks on one interfacing panel; then cut them apart after stitching. Simply stitch on the grid lines within the blocks, then cut on the grid lines between the blocks.

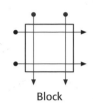

Block

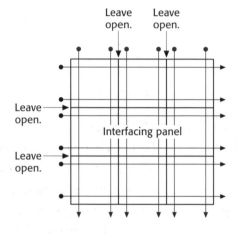

Interfacing panel

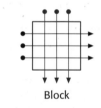

Block

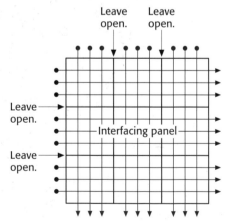

Combine several blocks on interfacing.

Preparing Grids

USING GRIDDED interfacing as a foundation makes it easier to place and sew pieces. The easiest option is to buy interfacing that has a grid printed on it, but there are other methods you might consider. You don't have to draw a grid on the interfacing at all, if you prefer. You can use the lines on your cutting mat (which should show through lightweight interfacing) to align the pieces. Another option is to prepare a paper template to use for multiple panels. Make a grid with dark, heavy lines the desired size, then lay the interfacing on top of it. The lines show through and you don't need to mark. I like to have a grid on the interfacing and recommend it to my students, but having a grid or not having a grid is your choice. Experiment and see what works for you.

Square Grids

Determine the number of pieces in your design that are required for height, width, and the unfinished square size. Lay the interfacing on the cutting mat with the fusible side down. Align the raw edges to best fit the needed width. If the interfacing is ½" short at the edges, it's still enough to secure the pieces. Just adjust the shortage evenly between both sides.

Draw a grid with a No. 2 pencil or water-soluble marker and clear ruler. Follow the lines on the mat carefully. Depending on the tip and angle of your marker, a grid can easily grow an extra ⅛" with each line you add. Back the ruler off the line, if necessary, to ensure an accurate grid. Space lines to match the size of your unfinished squares. Draw the vertical lines, then turn and add the horizontal lines. Align the previously drawn lines with the mat to ensure that the grid will be square.

Equilateral Triangle Grids

Equilateral triangles are triangles that have 60-degree angles in each corner. To prepare a triangular grid, three sets of lines are needed. Read over the general information in "Preparing Grids" and "Square Grids" above, then use the following procedure to draw the lines.

Draw the first set of lines either vertically or horizontally. If you cut 3"-wide strips of fabric to cut into triangles, draw lines every 3". Next, align the 60-degree line of your ruler on one of the marked lines. Draw a 60-degree line marker. Turn the interfacing and align the ruler with the 60-degree line marker and the mat lines. Now draw a second set of lines the width of your strips. For the final set of grid lines, rotate the ruler and align the two intersecting 60-degree lines of the ruler with the intersecting drawn lines. Draw a 60-degree line marker. Turn the interfacing and align the ruler with the marker line and the mat lines. Now draw the final set of lines the width of your strips.

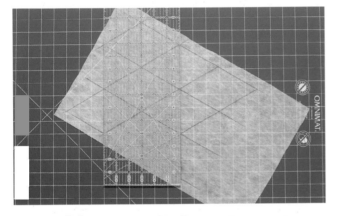

Draw triangle grids, maintaining 60-degree angles

To assist in matching triangle points when stitching, mark points where the ¼" seams will intersect. Using the Six-Arm Template above right, or another marking tool, align the center of each arm with the grid lines on the interfacing and place a dot on the interfacing at each triangle corner.

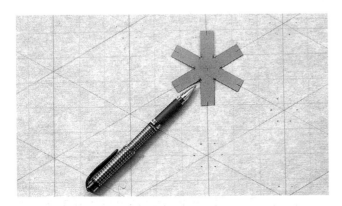

Twist the point of a mechanical pencil to mark
¼" seam intersections.

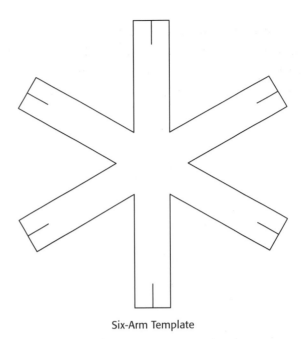

Six-Arm Template

Joining Interfacing Panels

When using printed interfacing, just cut the grid to the size you need. If the interfacing isn't large enough, align two pieces and lightly steam-baste them with the tip of the iron to make a larger piece. Trim away the excess, leaving ½" overlap. Be careful not to fuse the interfacing to the iron or the ironing board. Or, you can lay out and fuse your quilt in sections, then join the sections traditionally.

Joining panels

Using Printed Grids and Fabric Pieces of Different Sizes

Students often wonder which interfacing to buy when the piece size or shape differs from the available printed grids. Will they need to mark their own grid? Not necessarily. Find a common measurement to align the pieces. For example, you can use a 2" grid for 3" squares. Simply work in increments of 6" (2" x 3" = 6"). Two 3" fabric squares will cover the same distance as three 2" squares across the grid, or 6". Or, a block of four 3" squares will cover the same surface area as a block of nine 2" squares. Begin by aligning the first square in one corner, then work out from the corner. Two adjacent sides of each square will align with the grid lines.

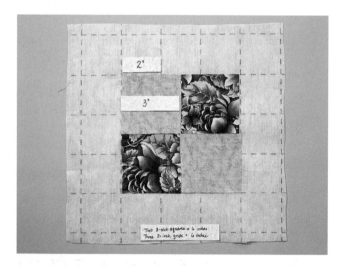

Four 3" fabric squares cover the same surface area as nine 2" squares on the grid.

Another example would be aligning a combination of squares and rectangles as in "Garland Irish Chain" on page 59. A 2½" square and a 6½" long rectangle combine to cover the distance of nine 1" squares on interfacing with a 1" grid as shown at top right.

Even triangles can be aligned with just a few hash marks on gridded fusible interfacing. For example, 3"-wide fabric strips cut into equilateral triangles with 3½" bases can be aligned by height within a 3" grid on interfacing. On the non-fusible side, pencil a mark

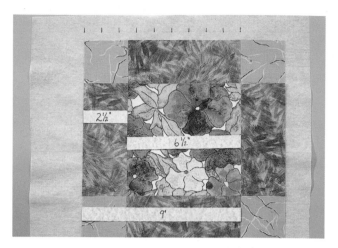

Positioning combinations of squares and rectangles

every 7" across the interfacing to align two 3½" triangle bases. Mark ¼" seam intersection dots as shown on page 23, after triangles are placed.

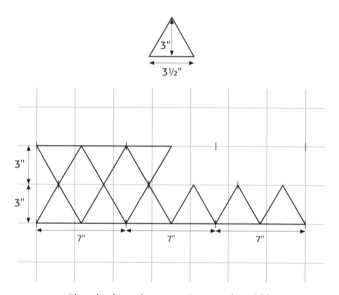

Place hash marks every 7" across the width of the interfacing to help align triangles.

Positioning triangles on a square grid

Fusing Designs

LAY THE interfacing on your work surface with the fusible side up. Check to be sure you've placed it properly. Position the watercolor pieces on the grid, right sides up. The fusible side of the interfacing will be fused to the wrong side of the fabrics.

Adjust the height of your ironing board to match the height of your work surface, then place the two next to each other. Gently pull a section of the interfacing panel onto the ironing board, then carefully line up pieces along the grid lines. With the iron on a medium steam setting, press firmly for ten seconds. Repeat, lifting and overlapping the previous section. Continue until the entire panel is fused.

You can peel off, re-position, and re-iron a piece if necessary, but do so only as a last resort. Removing a securely fused piece may distort or tear the bonding agent.

Allow the fabric to cool, then check the bond. Re-press as needed to ensure that there are no loose edges.

When working on quilts that are larger than my table, I design a section, fuse, and then design the next section. An alternative is to lay out the quilt top on a design wall, then transfer it in sections to the interfacing.

Piecing Square and Rectangular Panels

TRADITIONAL WATERCOLOR piecing involves sewing a square to a square to form rows, then joining the rows. Fused watercolor designs allow you to skip the square-to-square piecing and jump straight to joining rows. You stitch vertical seams, clip at the intersections, then stitch horizontal seams. Aligning the raw edges of individual squares is taken care of when the pieces are fused.

Piecing a 122-square watercolor design with traditional methods would require 120 seams. Fusing the same design to an interfacing foundation requires only 20 seams. Another bonus is that you don't need to worry about mixing up the squares or rotating

them. After they've been fused, you can stitch the panel with confidence.

1. Fold the panel along grid lines, right sides together. Sew the longest seams first, stitching a scant ¼" from the folds. The grid line is the fold line, not the stitching line. Stitch carefully so the panel doesn't pull to one side at the beginning or end of a row—you don't want the long seam to curve.

   Interfacing panels usually curl in on themselves as you sew. Be careful not to catch the edges of the panel as you stitch the second and third rows of the design.

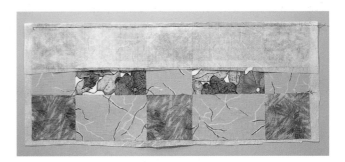

Sew longest seams first.

2. At each grid intersection, clip through the seam allowances to the stitching line. The ¼" snip will allow you to finger-press the seam allowances in opposite directions in the next step. Clip each intersection along each row. Do not cut the rows apart.

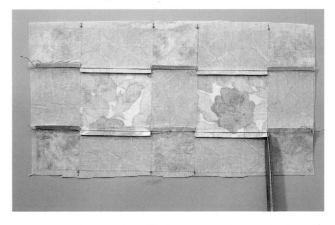

Clip rows.

3. Fold the panel along the unstitched grid lines. Finger-press seam allowances in opposite directions. Pressing in opposite directions creates snug intersections and prevents "speed bumps" from forming.

4. Stitch the remaining rows using a scant ¼" seam allowance and pulling the quilt top slightly as you sew the seam. As you stitch, feel carefully with a fingertip to make sure that seam allowances are positioned correctly before they go under the needle.

Stitch remaining seams.

5. Press the panel from the back first, pressing all seam allowances in one direction.

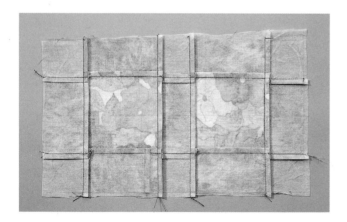

Press from the back.

6. Clip threads and any twisted seam allowances. Check your iron for any interfacing residue and clean it if necessary. Use a press cloth when in doubt. Turn the panel over and press from the front; use steam and press well so seam allowances lie flat.

Piecing Triangle Panels

PIECING TRIANGLES will align six intersecting points with three sets of seams. Triangle panels are pieced in the same manner as squares and rectangles with one exception. The triangle points are marked on the interfacing grid to make matching the points and aligning seam lines easier (see the design of equilateral triangles on page 21 and "Equilateral Triangle Grids" on page 22.) The interfacing will stabilize any bias edges and allow you to see the finished fabric combination.

1. Fold the panel along grid lines in the longest direction, right sides together, pinning at the dots. Beginning ¼" from the fold at the marked dot, stitch to the dot at the end of the first triangle. Stitch carefully so the panel doesn't pull to one side.

2. Lift your presser foot and pull the panel through without breaking the threads. Begin stitching at the next dot and continue along the base of the triangle to the dot at the other side. Repeat, stitching from dot to dot for each triangle to complete the row.

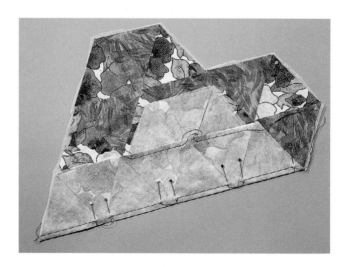

Stitch first set of rows from dot to dot.

3. At each grid intersection clip through the stitched seams as far as the marked dot in two directions. The ½" snip will allow you to line up the triangle corners and finger-press the seam allowances in opposite directions in the steps that follow. Double-clip each intersection along each row. Do not cut the rows apart.

Double-clip rows.

4. Fold the panel along the unstitched grid lines in a second direction; leave the rows in the shortest direction for the final step. Moving the seam allowances out of the way, stitch the rows in the second direction as with the first set of rows.

Stitch second set of rows from dot to dot.

5. Fold the panel along the remaining unstitched grid lines and pin. To achieve intersections that lie absolutely flat, follow these pressing directions carefully. Open seam allowances and place a positioning pin through the dots. In the first row, finger-press the top and bottom pairs of seam allowances in opposite directions, and alternate the directions at each set of seam intersections. For example, press the first top pair of seam allowances up and the bottom pair down, the next top pair of seam allowances down and the bottom pair up, and the next top pair of seam allowances up and bottom pair down. Continue in this manner along the entire length of the row.

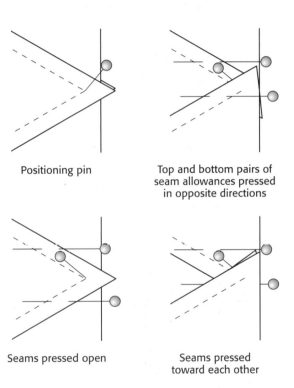

Positioning pin

Top and bottom pairs of seam allowances pressed in opposite directions

Seams pressed open

Seams pressed toward each other

In the second row, alternate pressing at each intersection again, but this time press one pair of seam allowances open and then press the next pair of seam allowances toward each other. For example, at the first seam intersection, finger-press the top pair of seam allowances open. Then press the bottom pair toward each other, tucking one side under the other. At the next seam intersection in the second row, press the top pair of seam allowances toward each other and the bottom pair open. Continue to alternate pressing along the entire length of the row.

Continue finger-pressing the entire panel in this same manner, pressing odd-numbered rows as described for the first row and even-numbered rows as described for the second row.

6. Stitch a few long machine basting stitches at each intersection to check matching. Remove basting and restitch if necessary. When you are happy with the matches, stitch the remaining rows using a ¼" seam allowance; use smaller stitches just over the intersections. Stitch completely to the edges for the last set of seam lines.

7. Clip points, threads, and any twisted seam allowances. Check your iron for any interfacing residue and clean it if necessary. Use a press cloth when in doubt. Turn the panel over and press from the front. Use steam and press well so star points swirl and seam allowances lie flat.

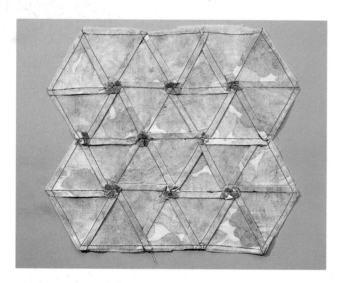

Press seam allowances carefully to minimize bulk.

Piecing Block Panels

GROUP BLOCKS with identical seaming on one piece of interfacing when possible. Stitch the long seams first, then clip the intersections along each row. Leave the seams open between the blocks. Complete the short seams, taking care to finger-press the seam allowances in opposite directions. Press well, then cut the blocks apart.

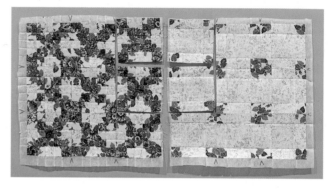

Place blocks with identical seaming on a single piece of interfacing.

Squaring Panels

IT IS important to have a square panel before joining panels to each other or adding borders. A few diagonal tugs may remedy some distortions. If necessary, square the panel by aligning center seams of the panel with the lines of a cutting mat, then align your ruler with each edge and trim the excess. A line of stay stitching less than ¼" from the edge will keep seam allowances from flipping and edges from stretching. Stipple quilting may help to hide or camouflage piecing imperfections.

Blooming Hedges

Blooming Hedges by Dina Pappas, 2000, Tecumseh, Michigan, 52½" x 52½".
Four watercolor blocks and a center square form this easy quilt, filling a center medallion with blooms.

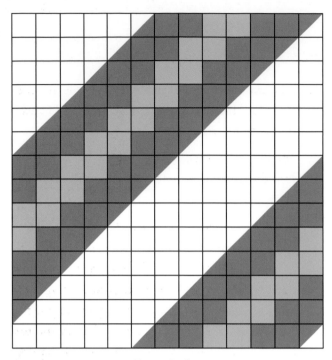

Finished Watercolor Panel: 19½" x 21"
Square Size: 2" x 2"

☐ Background (need 280)

◹ Edge (need 112)

◼ Full-floral 1 (need 224)

◼ Full-floral 2 (need 112)

Master Design
Use the master design as a guide.
Vary the design as necessary for a realistic look.

Materials

42"-wide fabric

- 1 yd. for background
- ½ yd. edge fabric
- 1 yd. full-floral fabric 1
- ½ yd. full-floral fabric 2
- ⅜ yd. for inner border
- ¾ yd. for outer border
- ¼ yd. for corner squares
- ½ yd. for binding
- 57" x 57" piece of batting
- 3⅜ yds. for backing
- 3⅛ yds. lightweight fusible interfacing, 44" wide

CUTTING CHART

Cut all strips across the width of the fabric unless otherwise indicated. Measurements include ¼" seam allowances. Note: If you vary your watercolor panel from the master design above, the pieces needed for each fabric will also vary.

Fabric	Number of Strips	Strip Size	Square Size	Pieces Needed
Background	14	2" x 42"	2"	280
Edge	6	2" x 42"	2"	113
Full-Floral 1	12	2" x 42"	2"	224
Full-Floral 2	6	2" x 42"	2"	112
Inner Border	4	2" x 42"		
Outer Border	4	5" x 42"		
Corner Squares	1	6½" x 42"	6½"	4
Binding	6	2½" x 42"		
Backing	2	42" x 57"*		

*Cut from the lengthwise grain of the fabric.

Designing

1. Cut the fusible interfacing into 3 pieces, each 26" x 28". Join 2 leftover pieces to form a fourth 26" x 28" piece. Following instructions for "Joining Interfacing Panels" on page 23, make four 13 x 14 grids of 2" squares.

2. Place an interfacing grid on your work surface, fusible side up. Following the master design on page 30, place the background and edge pieces on the interfacing grid. Be sure to use 13 squares across the top and 14 squares along the side.

3. Fill in the remaining grid with full-floral squares, using full-floral fabrics 1 and 2 as indicated in the master design. To build complete flowers, place squares so the edges echo the colors of adjacent squares.

4. Evaluate your design. Look for a smooth transition between full-floral fabrics 1 and 2. Make adjustments by replacing or rotating squares as needed.

5. After the watercolor panel is complete, straighten the pieces on the grid. Fuse the squares in place, following the instructions for "Fusing Designs" on page 25.

6. Make the remaining 3 panels in the same manner as the first. Arrange the 4 panels to form the pattern shown in the photo on page 29. Align the outside edges of the blocks, leaving space in the center for 1 square. Choose a center square to best complement the 4 panels. Make any final adjustments to blend the panel intersections by replacing or rotating squares.

Stitching

1. Sew the panels together, following the instructions for "Piecing Square and Rectangular Panels" on pages 25–26. Press well.

2. Square the finished panels to 20" x 21½", following the instructions for "Squaring Panels" on page 28.

3. Arrange the watercolor panels and the center square to form the pattern. Place the center square, right sides together, over bottom right corner of the top left Blooming Hedges panel. Using a ¼" seam allowance, join the center square to panel 1 with a partial seam. Beginning ½" from the top of the square, sew to the bottom of the square. Finger-press the seam allowance toward the panel.

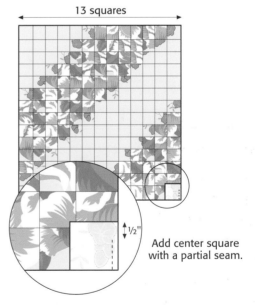

13 squares

½"

Add center square with a partial seam.

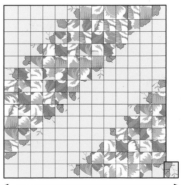

13 squares plus center

4. Working counterclockwise around the center square, join the remaining panels, matching seams and easing as necessary.

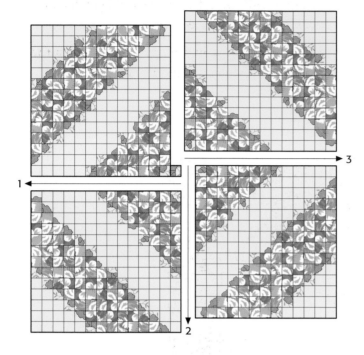

5. Fold the last panel added, right sides together, over panel 1. Complete the partial seam on the center square and join the remaining panels, matching seams and easing as necessary.

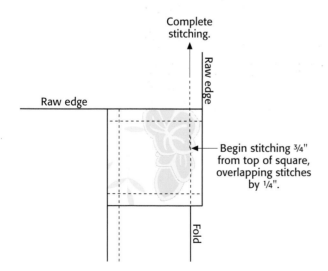

Adding Borders

1. Join each 2" x 42" inner border strip to each 5" x 42" outer border strip. Press seams toward the darker fabric.

2. Measure quilt top horizontally through the center. From 2 border strips, cut 2 pieces to the measured length. Stitch the corner squares to the ends of each strip. Press the seam allowances toward the border strips.

3. Measure the quilt top vertically through the center. From 2 border strips, cut 2 pieces to the measured length. Sew the border strips to the side edges of the quilt top, pressing the seam allowances toward the borders.

4. Sew the border strips with corner squares to the top and bottom edges of the quilt. Press the seam allowances toward the border.

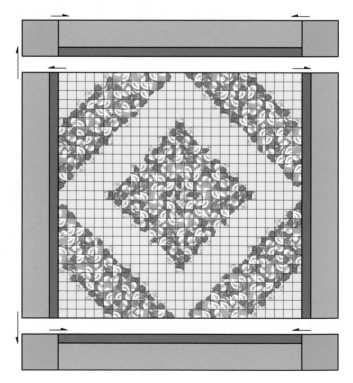

Quilting Suggestions and Finishing

NOTE: *For general quilting instructions and help with specific techniques, refer to "Finishing Techniques" on pages 88–95.*

1. Piece the backing fabric and trim to 57" x 57". Layer the backing, batting, and quilt top. Pin-baste the quilt sandwich.

2. If you want to follow my quilting plan, proceed as follows: Stipple-quilt the background areas and meander-quilt through the floral areas, stitching around individual flowers to highlight blooms. Quilt the borders as desired.

3. Referring to "Binding" on pages 93–95, join the binding strips and sew them to the quilt top.

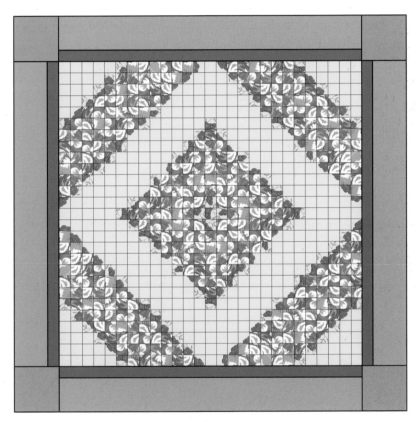

Quilt Plan

Two-Color Blooming Hedges

Two-Color Blooming Hedges by Dina Pappas, 2000, Tecumseh, Michigan, 52½" x 52½".
Rotating the panels in the Blooming Hedges design changes the setting, replacing the center floral medallion with the solid background corners. The plain areas become the perfect spaces for more flowers, this time done in appliqué.

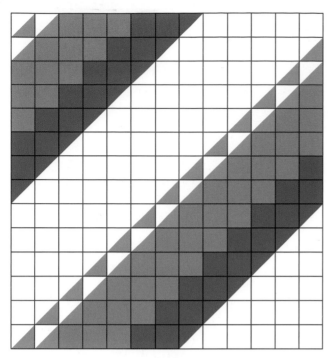

Finished Watercolor Panel: 19½" x 21"
Square Size: 2" x 2"

☐ Background (need 280)

◪ Edge 1 (need 56)

◪ Edge 2 (need 112)*

◼ Full-floral 1 (need 112)

◼ Full-floral 2 (need 168)

*This fabric is represented by a large diagonal shape in the master design at left. Substitute other edge shapes as necessary for a smooth transition between fabrics. See "Basic Edge Shapes" on pages 17–18.

Master Design
Use the master design as a guide.
Vary the design as necessary for a realistic look.

CUTTING CHART

Cut all strips across the width of the fabric unless otherwise indicated. Measurements include ¼" seam allowances. Note: If you vary your watercolor panel from the master design above, the pieces needed for each fabric will also vary.

Fabric	Number of Strips	Strip Size	Square Size	Pieces Needed
Background	14	2" x 42"	2"	281
Edge 1	3	2" x 42"	2"	56
Full-Floral 1	6	2" x 42"	2"	112
Full-Floral 2	9	2" x 42"	2"	168
Edge 2	6	2" x 42"	2"	112
Inner Border	4	2" x 42"		
Outer Border	4	5" x 42"		
Corner Squares	1	6½" x 42"	6½"	4
Binding	6	2½" x 42"		
Backing	2	42" x 57" *		

*Cut from the lengthwise grain of the fabric.

Materials

42"-wide fabric

- 1 yd. for background
- ¼ yd. edge fabric 1
- ½ yd. full-floral fabric 1
- ⅝ yd. full-floral fabric 2
- ½ yd. edge fabric 2
- ½ yd. total assorted green fabrics for leaf and branch appliqués
- ½ yd. total assorted fabrics for flower appliqués (6" dark rose, 4" medium rose, and 4" purple)
- ⅜ yd. for inner border
- ¾ yd. for outer border
- ¼ yd. for corner squares
- ½ yd. for binding
- 57" x 57" piece of batting
- 3⅜ yds. for backing
- 3⅛ yds. lightweight fusible interfacing, 44" wide
- Freezer paper

Designing

1. Cut the fusible interfacing into 3 pieces, each 26" x 28". Join 2 leftover pieces to make a fourth 26" x 28" piece. Using one of the methods outlined in "Preparing Grids" on page 22, make four 13 x 14 grids of 2" squares.

2. Place an interfacing grid on your work surface, fusible side up. Following the master design on page 35, place the background and squares of edge fabrics 1 and 2 on the interfacing grid. Be sure to use 13 squares across the top and 14 squares along the side.

3. Fill in the remaining grid with full-floral squares, using full-floral fabrics 1 and 2 as indicated in the master design. To build complete flowers, place squares so the edges echo the colors of adjacent squares.

4. Evaluate your design. Look for a smooth transition between full-floral fabrics 1 and 2 and edge fabrics 1 and 2. Make adjustments by replacing or rotating squares as needed.

5. After the watercolor panel is complete, straighten the pieces on the grid. Fuse the squares in place, following the instructions for "Fusing Designs" on page 25.

6. Make the remaining 3 panels in the same manner as the first. Arrange the 4 panels to form the pattern shown in the photo on page 34. Align the outside edges of the blocks, leaving space in the center for 1 square. Choose a center square to best complement the 4 panels. Make any final adjustments to blend the panel intersections by replacing or rotating squares.

Stitching

1. Sew the panels together, following the instructions for "Piecing Square and Rectangular Panels" on pages 25–26. Press well.

2. Square the finished panels to 20" x 21½", following the instructions for "Squaring Panels" on page 28.

Appliqué

1. Following "Freezer-Paper Appliqué" steps 1–4 on page 83, trace the appliqué template patterns on pages 39–40 onto freezer paper and prepare the appliqué pieces.

2. Join the pieces to form flower units as indicated by the templates. Arrange the flower units and branches on the panels as shown in the photo on page 34. Continue as described in steps 5 and 6 of "Freezer-Paper Appliqué" on pages 83–84.

Joining Panels

1. Arrange the watercolor panels and the center square to form the pattern. Place the center square, right sides together, over the bottom right corner of the top left Two-Color Blooming Hedges panel. Using a ¼" seam allowance, join the center square to panel 1 with a partial seam. Beginning ½" from the top of the square, sew to the bottom of the square. Finger-press the seam allowance toward the panel.

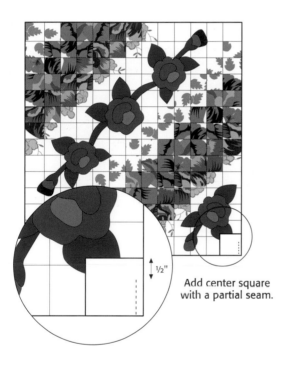

½"

Add center square with a partial seam.

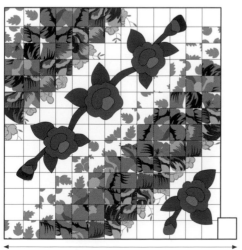

13 squares plus center

2. Working counterclockwise around the center square, join the remaining panels, matching seams and easing as necessary.

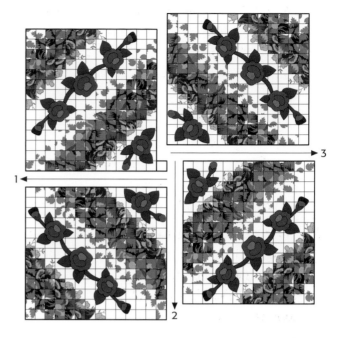

3. Fold the last panel added, right sides together, over panel 1. Complete the partial seam on the center square and join the remaining panels, matching seams and easing as necessary.

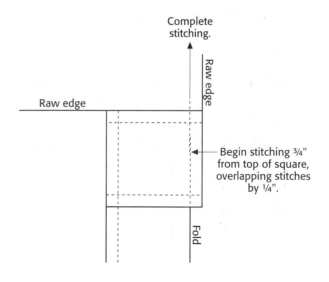

Complete stitching.

Raw edge

Raw edge

Begin stitching ¾" from top of square, overlapping stitches by ¼".

Fold

Adding Borders

1. Join each 2" x 42" inner border strip to each 5" x 42" outer border strip. Press seam allowances toward the darker fabric.

2. Measure the quilt top horizontally through the center. From 2 border strips, cut 2 pieces to the measured length. Stitch the corner squares to the ends of each strip, pressing the seam allowances toward the border strips.

3. Measure the quilt top vertically through the center. From 2 border strips, cut 2 pieces to the measured length. Sew the border strips to the side edges of the quilt top, pressing the seam allowances toward the borders.

4. Sew the border strips with corner squares to the top and bottom edges of the quilt. Press the seam allowances toward the border.

Quilting Suggestions and Finishing

NOTE: *For general quilting instructions and help with specific techniques, refer to "Finishing Techniques" on page 88–95.*

1. Piece the backing fabric and trim to 57" x 57". Layer the backing, batting, and quilt top. Pin-baste the quilt sandwich.

2. If you want to follow my quilting plan, proceed as follows: Stipple-quilt the background areas and meander-quilt through the floral areas, stitching around individual flowers to highlight blooms. Add detail quilting on appliqués, such as veins on leaves and flowers. Quilt the borders as desired.

3. Referring to "Binding" on pages 93–95, join the binding strips and sew them to the quilt top.

Two-Color Blooming Hedges
Appliqué Patterns

*Identical pieces are labeled with
the same number in all flower units.*

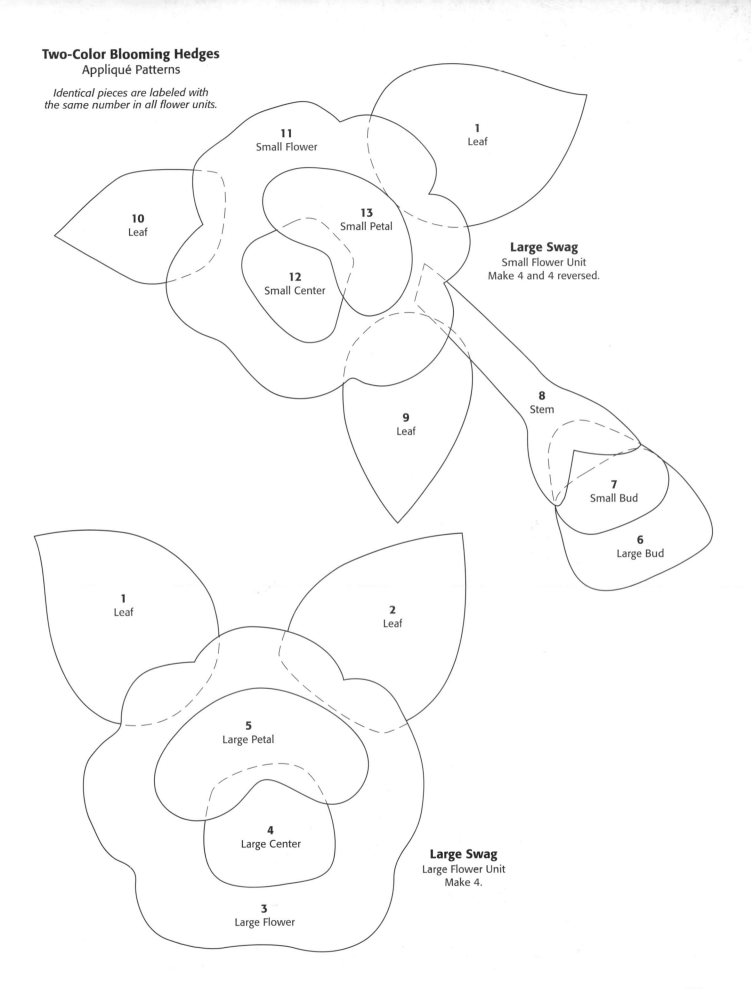

11
Small Flower

1
Leaf

10
Leaf

13
Small Petal

12
Small Center

Large Swag
Small Flower Unit
Make 4 and 4 reversed.

9
Leaf

8
Stem

7
Small Bud

6
Large Bud

1
Leaf

2
Leaf

5
Large Petal

4
Large Center

Large Swag
Large Flower Unit
Make 4.

3
Large Flower

Two-Color Blooming Hedges
Appliqué Patterns

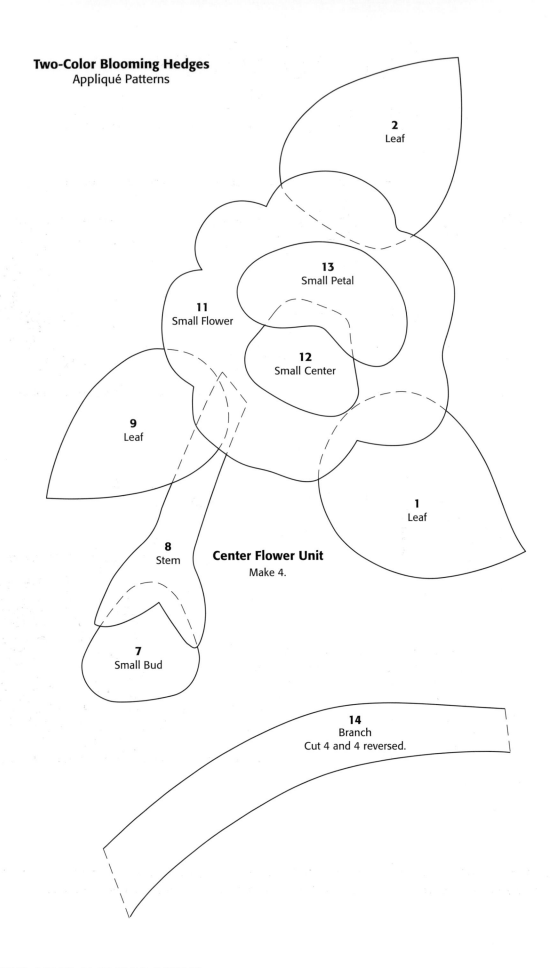

2
Leaf

13
Small Petal

11
Small Flower

12
Small Center

9
Leaf

1
Leaf

8
Stem

Center Flower Unit
Make 4.

7
Small Bud

14
Branch
Cut 4 and 4 reversed.

Twined Vines
Runner and Place Mats

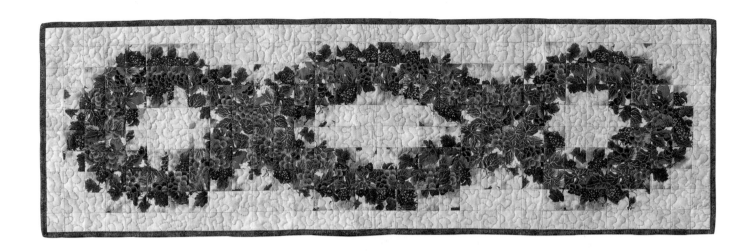

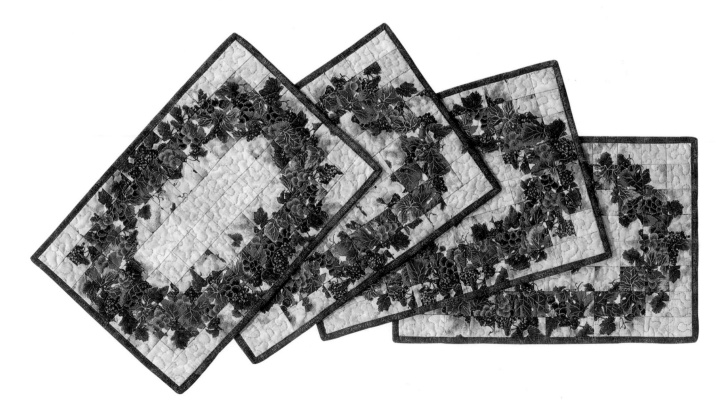

Twined Vines Runner and Place Mats by Dina Pappas, 2000, Colbert, Washington, 15" x 48" runner, 12" x 18" place mats.
Make your table the center of attention with this colorful table runner and coordinating place mats.

Finished Runner: 15" x 48"
Square Size: 2" x 2"

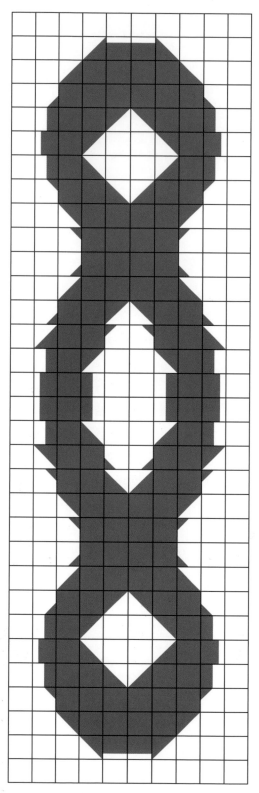

Background (need 124)

Large diagonal (need 44)

Small diagonal (need 24)

Full edge (need 12)

Half edge (need 16)

Full floral (need 100)

Master Design
Use the master design as a guide.
Vary the design as necessary for a realistic look.

Finished Place Mat: 12" x 18"
Square Size: 2" x 2"

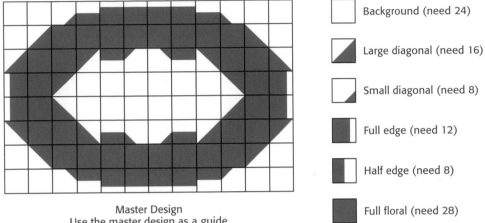

Master Design
Use the master design as a guide.
Vary the design as necessary for a realistic look.

- ☐ Background (need 24)
- ◺ Large diagonal (need 16)
- ◹ Small diagonal (need 8)
- ▮ Full edge (need 12)
- ▯ Half edge (need 8)
- ▮ Full floral (need 28)

CUTTING CHART

Cut all strips across the width of the fabric. Measurements include ¼" seam allowances. Note: If you vary your watercolor panels from the master design above and on the facing page, the pieces needed for each fabric will also vary.

Fabric	Number of Strips	Strip Size	Square Size	Pieces Needed
Background	11	2" x 42"	2"	220
Edge	14	2" x 42"	2"	272
Full Floral	11	2" x 42"	2"	212
Binding	10	2½" x 42"		

Materials

42"-wide fabric

- ¾ yd. for background
- 1 yd. edge fabric
- ¾ yd. full-floral fabric
- ⅞ yd. for binding
- 41" x 64" piece of batting
- 1⅞ yds. for backing
- 1⅞ yds. lightweight fusible interfacing, 44" wide

Designing the Runner

1. Cut the fusible interfacing as illustrated with 1 piece 20" x 64" and 4 pieces 24" x 16". Using one of the methods outlined in "Preparing Grids" on page 22, make one 10 x 32 grid and four 8 x 12 grids of 2" squares.

2. Place the large interfacing grid on your work surface, fusible side up. Following the master design for the runner on page 42, place the background pieces on the interfacing grid.

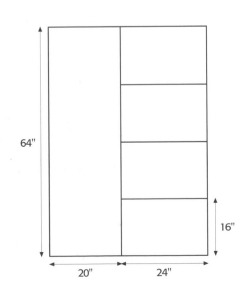

64"

16"

20"

24"

3. Gather edge squares that resemble the illustrations below, then use them to create the edges of the vine. For tips on placing squares, refer to "Placing Edge Pieces" on pages 18–19.

Large diagonal
Need 44.

Small diagonal
Need 24.

Full edge
Need 12.

Half edge
Need 16.

4. Fill in the remaining grid with full-floral fabrics. To build complete flowers, place squares so the edges echo the colors of adjacent squares.

5. Evaluate your design. Look for smooth curves. Make adjustments by replacing or rotating squares as needed.

6. After the watercolor panel is complete, straighten the pieces on the grid. Fuse the squares in place, following the instructions for "Fusing Designs" on page 25.

Lengthen the runner by adding another center oval or stretching each oval by adding identical rows in the center of each of three ovals. An extra ¾ yard of interfacing and ⅜ yard each of background, edge, and full-floral fabrics would increase the runner length by 13 squares to 67½" and yield another pair of place mats.

Designing the Place Mats

1. Place a 16" x 24" interfacing grid on your work surface, fusible side up. Following the master design for the place mat on page 43, place the background pieces on the interfacing grid.

2. Gather edge squares that resemble the illustrations below, then use them to create the inside and outside edges of the ovals. For tips on placing squares, refer to "Placing Edge Pieces" on pages 18–19.

Large diagonal
Need 16.

Small diagonal
Need 8.

Full edge
Need 12.

Half edge
Need 8.

3. Fill in the remaining grid with full-floral squares. To build complete flowers, place squares so the edges and corners echo the colors of adjacent squares.

4. Evaluate your design. Look for smooth curves. Make adjustments by replacing or rotating squares as needed.

5. After the watercolor panel is complete, straighten the pieces on the grid. Fuse the squares in place, following the instructions for "Fusing Designs" on page 25.

6. Make 3 additional place mats, following the place mat master design.

Stitching

1. Sew the panels together, following the instructions for "Piecing Square and Rectangular Panels" on pages 25–26. Press well.

2. Square the finished runner to 15½" x 48½" and the finished place mat panels to 12½" x 18½", following the instructions for "Squaring Panels" on page 28.

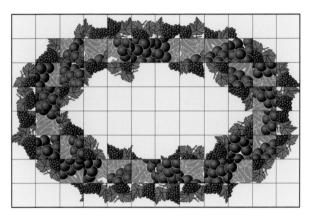

Place mat

Quilting Suggestions and Finishing

NOTE: *For general quilting instructions and help with specific techniques, refer to "Finishing Techniques" on pages 88–95.*

1. Trim the backing fabric to 41" x 64". Layer the backing, batting, and quilt tops. Pin-baste the quilt sandwiches. Cut apart the runner and place mat sandwiches.

2. If you want to follow my quilting plan, proceed as follows: Stipple-quilt the background areas and meander-quilt through the floral areas, stitching around individual flowers to highlight blooms.

3. Referring to "Binding" on pages 93–95, join the binding strips and sew them to the runner and place mats.

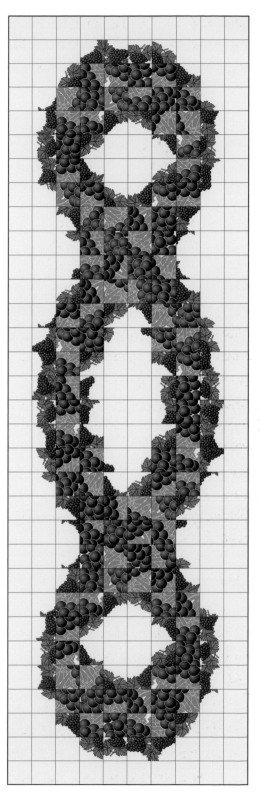

Table runner

Lacy Eight-Pointed Star
Wall Hanging

Lacy Eight-Pointed Star of Pansies by Dina Pappas, 2000, Eagle River, Alaska, 53½" x 53½".
Open areas were added to the star to create a lacy, cutwork look.

Finished Watercolor Panel: 33" x 33"
Square Size: 2" x 2"

Background
(need 212)

Large diagonal
(need 72)

Small diagonal
(need 16)

Full edge
(need 32)

Half edge
(need 28)

Valley
(need 12)

Full floral
(need 112)

Master Design
Use the master design as a guide.
Vary the design as necessary for a realistic look.

Corner Block Finished Size: 4" x 4"

Materials

42"-wide fabric

- ¾ yd. for background
- ⅝ yd. edge fabric
- ½ yd. full-floral fabric
- ⅞ yd. light green for border and corner blocks
- ¾ yd. fuchsia for border and corner blocks
- 1¼ yds. purple for border and corner blocks
- ½ yd. for binding
- 57" x 57" piece of batting
- 3½ yds. for backing
- 1⅜ yds. lightweight fusible interfacing, 44" wide

CUTTING CHART

Cut all strips across the width of the fabric unless otherwise indicated. Measurements include ¼" seam allowances. Note: If you vary your watercolor panel from the master design on page 47, the pieces needed for each fabric will also vary.

Fabric	Number of Strips	Strip Size	Square Size	Pieces Needed
Background	11	2" x 42"	2"	212
Edge	8	2" x 42"	2"	160
Full Floral	12	2" x 42"	2"	112
Light green				
(corner blocks)	1	2½" x 42"	2½"	12
(corner blocks)	1	3" x 42"	3"	12
(border)	4	4½" x 42"		
Fuchsia				
(corner blocks)	4	1½" x 42"		
(border)	5	2" x 42"		
Purple				
(corner blocks)	4	1½" x 42"		
(border)	6	5" x 42"		
Binding	6	2½" x 42"		
Backing	2	42" x 57" *		

*Cut from the lengthwise grain of the fabric.

Designing

1. Cut the fusible interfacing into a 44" x 44" square. Using one of the methods outlined in "Preparing Grids" on page 22, make a 22 x 22 grid of 2" squares.

2. Place the interfacing grid on your work surface, fusible side up. Following the master design on page 47, place the background squares on the interfacing grid.

3. Gather edge squares that resemble the illustrations below, then use them to create the outer and inner edges of the star. For tips on placing squares, refer to "Placing Edge Pieces" on pages 18–19.

Large diagonal
Need 72.

Small diagonal
Need 16.

Full edge
Need 32.

Half edge
Need 28.

Valley
Need 12.

4. Fill in the remaining grid with full-floral squares. To build complete flowers, place squares so the edges echo the colors of adjacent squares.

5. Evaluate your design. Make adjustments by replacing or rotating squares as needed. Be prepared to cut a few more squares if necessary.

Stitching

1. After the watercolor panel is complete, straighten the pieces on the grid. Fuse the squares in place, following the instructions for "Fusing Designs" on page 25.

2. Sew the panel together, following the instructions for "Piecing Square and Rectangular Panels" on pages 25–26. Press well.

3. Square the finished panels to 33½" x 33½", following the instructions for "Squaring Panels" on page 28.

Corner Block Assembly

1. Join the long edges of the 1½" fuchsia and purple strips. Press the seam allowances open. Make 4 strip sets. Using the diamond template pattern on page 50, cut 6 diamonds from each strip set, aligning the template centerline with the seam between colors.

2. Cut twelve 2½" light green squares in half once diagonally to make 24 small triangles. Cut twelve 3" light green squares in half once diagonally to make 24 large triangles.

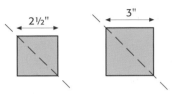

3. Join a small triangle to the fuchsia side of a diamond. Join a large triangle to the purple side of the diamond to form unit A.

Unit A
Make 12.

4. Join a small triangle to the purple side of a diamond. Join a large triangle to the fuchsia side of the diamond to form unit B.

Unit B
Make 12.

5. Join 1 unit A to 1 unit B along the diagonal edges to form a corner block. Make 12 blocks.

Corner Block
Make 12.

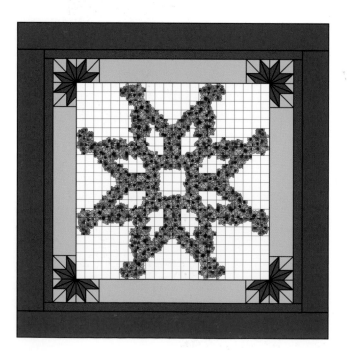

Adding Borders

1. Measure the quilt top horizontally and vertically through the center. Subtract 8" and cut 4 light green strips to the determined length.

2. Sew a corner block to each end of 2 strips, then sew these border strips to the sides of the quilt. Sew 2 corner blocks to each end of the remaining 2 strips as shown, then sew the border strips to the top and bottom of the quilt. Press the seam allowances toward the border.

Make 2 for side borders.

Make 2 for top and bottom borders.

3. Join the 2" fuchsia border strips and add the borders, following the instructions for "Straight-Cut Borders" on pages 85–86. Repeat for the 5" purple border strips.

Quilting Suggestions and Finishing

NOTE: *For general quilting instructions and help with specific techniques, refer to "Finishing Techniques" on pages 88–95.*

1. Piece the backing fabric, then trim to 57" x 57". Layer the backing, batting, and quilt top. Pin-baste the quilt sandwich.

2. If you want to follow my quilting plan, proceed as follows: Stipple-quilt the background areas and meander-quilt through the floral areas, stitching around individual flowers to highlight blooms. Quilt borders as desired.

3. Referring to "Binding" on pages 93–95, join the binding strips and sew them to the quilt top.

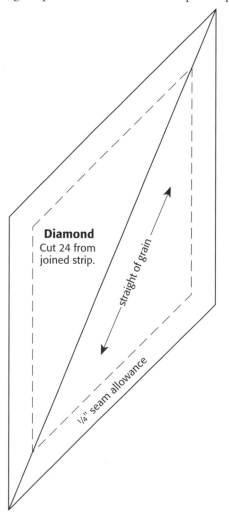

Diamond
Cut 24 from joined strip.

straight of grain

¼" seam allowance

Garden Sampler

Garden Sampler by Dina Pappas, 2000, Tecumseh, Michigan, 53½" x 70".
A bright scrappy border frames various garden scenes, adding a fresh look to the quilt.
The checked border is sewn with the blocks, making piecing a breeze.

Finished Watercolor Panel: 43½" x 60"
Square Size: 2" x 2"

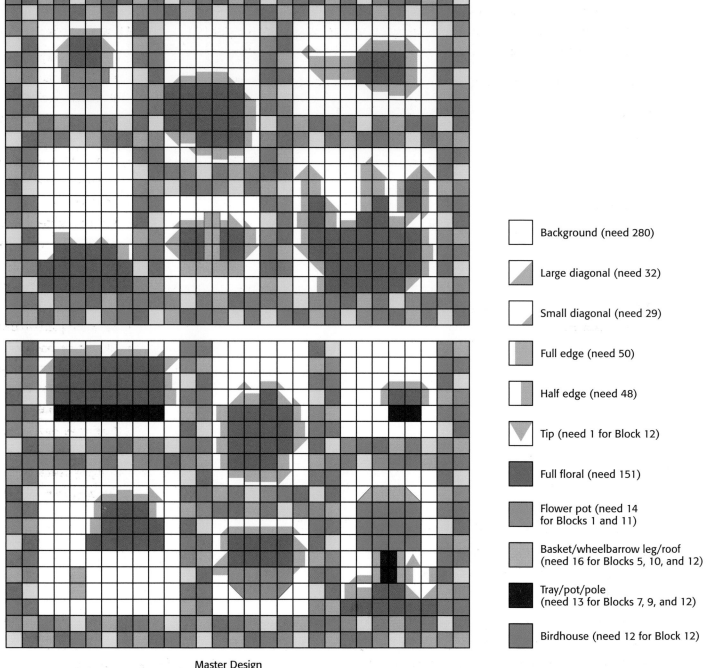

Background (need 280)

Large diagonal (need 32)

Small diagonal (need 29)

Full edge (need 50)

Half edge (need 48)

Tip (need 1 for Block 12)

Full floral (need 151)

Flower pot (need 14 for Blocks 1 and 11)

Basket/wheelbarrow leg/roof (need 16 for Blocks 5, 10, and 12)

Tray/pot/pole (need 13 for Blocks 7, 9, and 12)

Birdhouse (need 12 for Block 12)

Master Design
Use the master design as a guide.
Vary the design as necessary for a realistic look.

Pieced Squares

Pieced from 1 flower pot and 1 background square (need 2 for Block 1)

Pieced from 1 flower pot and 1 background square (need 2 for Block 11)

Pieced from 1 basket and 1 edge square (need 1 for Block 5)

Pieced from 1 basket and 1 edge square (need 1 for Block 5)

Pieced from 1 basket and 1 floral square (need 4 for Block 5)

Pieced from 1 roof and 1 background square (need 2 for Block 12)

Pieced from 1 pole and 1 edge square (need 4 for Block 12)

CUTTING CHART

Cut all strips across the width of the fabric unless otherwise indicated. Measurements include ¼" seam allowances. Note: If you vary your watercolor panel from the master design on the facing page, the pieces needed for each fabric will also vary.

Fabric	Number of Strips	Strip Size	Square Size	Pieces Needed
Background	14	2" x 42"	2"	277
Edge	9	2" x 42"	2"	165
Full Floral	8	2" x 42"	2"	149
Scrap border (each color)	5	2" x 42"	2"	530
Outer Border	2	5½" x 60½" *		
	2	5½" x 53½" *		
Binding	7	2½" x 42"		
Backing	2	42" x 58" *		

*Cut from the lengthwise grain of the fabric.

Materials

42"-wide fabric

- 1 yd. for background
- ⅝ yd. edge fabric
- ⅝ yd. full-floral fabric
- ⅜ yd. each of 6 fabrics for scrap border
- ½ yd. total assorted fabrics for containers and appliqués
- Scrap of printed fabric with butterfly and other insect motifs for appliqué
- 1⅞ yds. for outer border
- ⅝ yd. for binding
- 58" x 75" piece of batting
- 3½ yds. for backing
- 3¼ yds. lightweight fusible interfacing, 44" wide
- Buttons to embellish birdhouse and clippers
- Ribbon to embellish hanging basket block
- Freezer paper

Designing

1. Cut the fusible interfacing into 2 pieces, one 58" x 42" and one 58" x 38". Using one of the methods outlined in "Preparing Grids" on page 22, make one 29 x 21 grid and one 29 x 19 grid of 2" squares.

2. Place the larger interfacing grid on your work surface, fusible side up. Following the top block of the master design on page 52, place the scrap border and background pieces on the interfacing grid. Leave pieced squares blank; they will be completed and filled in later.

If your work surface is too small for the panel, then work in sections. Design a few blocks and border, then fuse.

3. Using edge squares, design the edges of the floral bouquets. For tips on placing squares, refer to "Placing Edge Pieces" on pages 18–19.

4. Except for the pieced squares, fill in the remaining grid with full-floral fabrics, following the master design. To build complete flowers, place squares so the edges echo the colors of adjacent squares.

5. Choose fabrics to make the flowerpot and basket. Cut 2" x 2" squares, 6 for the flowerpot and 10 for the basket. Fold 2 flowerpot squares and 6 basket squares in half lengthwise, wrong sides together. Lightly press a crease to use as a stitching guide. Place each flower pot square over a background square, place 4 basket squares over full-floral squares, and place the 2 remaining basket squares over half-edge squares. For each pair of layered squares, stitch along the crease. Trim ¼" away from the stitching on one side and press open to make the squares indicated in the master design on page 52. Place the pieced squares on the interfacing grid.

6. Evaluate your design. Make adjustments by replacing or rotating squares as needed. Be prepared to cut a few more squares if necessary.

7. After the watercolor panel is complete, straighten the pieces on the grid. Fuse the squares in place following the instructions for "Fusing Designs" on page 25.

8. Make the remaining panel, following the bottom block design on page 52. Choose fabrics and cut 2" x 2" squares to make pots, wheelbarrow leg, birdhouse, and birdhouse roof and pole. Fold 4 pole squares in half lengthwise, wrong sides together. Lightly press a crease to use as a stitching guide. Place each pole square over an edge square and stitch along the crease. Trim ¼" away from the stitching on one side and press open. Place the squares on the interfacing grid.

9. Fold 2 flower pot squares and 2 birdhouse roof squares in half diagonally, wrong sides together. Lightly press a crease to use as a stitching guide. Layer each square right sides together with a background square. Stitch along the crease. Trim ¼" away from the stitching on one side and press open. Place the half-square triangles on the interfacing grid. After the watercolor panel is complete, straighten the pieces on the grid. Fuse the squares in place, following the instructions for "Fusing Designs" on page 25.

Stitching

1. Sew the panels, following the instructions for "Piecing Square and Rectangular Panels" on pages 25–26. Press well.

2. Following steps 1–4 in "Freezer-Paper Appliqué" on page 83, use the templates on pages 56–58 to trace shapes 1–13 onto freezer paper, and prepare the appliqué pieces.

3. Pin the pieces in place on the grid. Using a large-eyed needle, thread the ribbon for the hanging basket; sew it over the hook, using the template as a placement guide. Continue as described in steps 5 and 6 in "Freezer-Paper Appliqué" on pages 83–84.

4. Trace reversed images of selected butterflies and other insects from printed fabric onto the unwaxed side of freezer paper and cut out. Fuse these images to the wrong side of fabric over matching butterflies and other insects. Continue as in steps 3–6 for "Freezer-Paper Appliqué" on pages 83–84.

5. Square the top finished panel to 44" x 32" and the bottom finished panel to 44" x 29", following the instructions for "Squaring Panels" on page 28. Join the panels as shown in the photo on page 51, matching seams and easing as necessary.

Quilt Assembly and Finishing

NOTE: *For general quilting instructions and help with specific techniques, refer to "Finishing Techniques" on pages 88–95.*

1. Referring to "Straight-Cut Borders" on pages 85–86, measure and sew the outer border strips to the side edges of the quilt top first, then to the top and bottom edges.

2. Piece the backing fabric, then trim to 58" x 74". Layer the backing, batting, and quilt top. Pin-baste the quilt sandwich.

3. If you want to follow my quilting plan, proceed as follows: Stipple-quilt the background areas and meander-quilt through the floral areas, stitching around individual flowers to highlight blooms. Add detail quilting to the flowerpots and other garden appliqués as desired. Embellish the birdhouse and clippers with buttons, securing with a machine zigzag stitch if desired.

4. Referring to "Binding" on pages 93–95, join the binding strips and sew them to the quilt top.

Quilt Plan

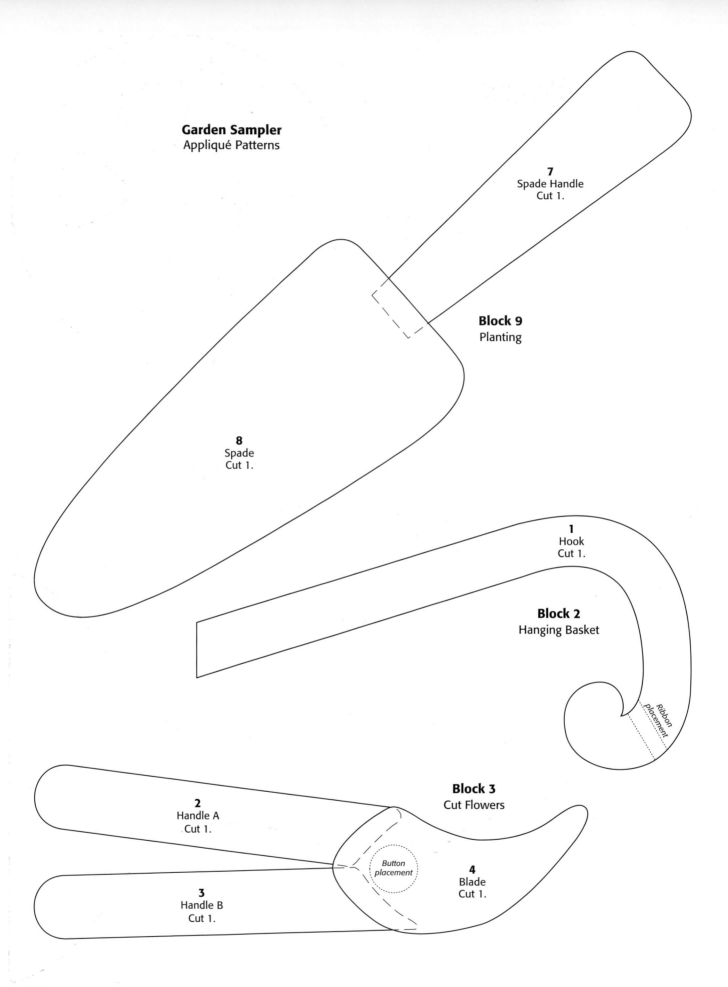

Garden Sampler
Appliqué Patterns

7
Spade Handle
Cut 1.

Block 9
Planting

8
Spade
Cut 1.

1
Hook
Cut 1.

Block 2
Hanging Basket

Ribbon placement

Block 3
Cut Flowers

2
Handle A
Cut 1.

Button placement

4
Blade
Cut 1.

3
Handle B
Cut 1.

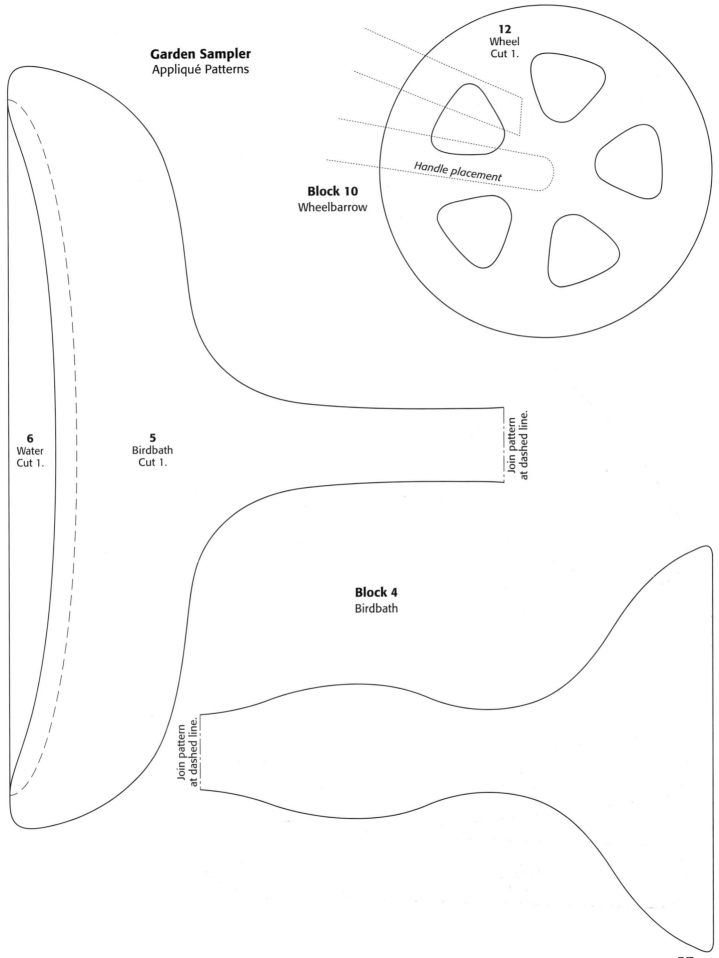

Garden Sampler
Appliqué Patterns

12
Wheel
Cut 1.

Block 10
Wheelbarrow

Handle placement

6
Water
Cut 1.

5
Birdbath
Cut 1.

Join pattern at dashed line.

Block 4
Birdbath

Join pattern at dashed line.

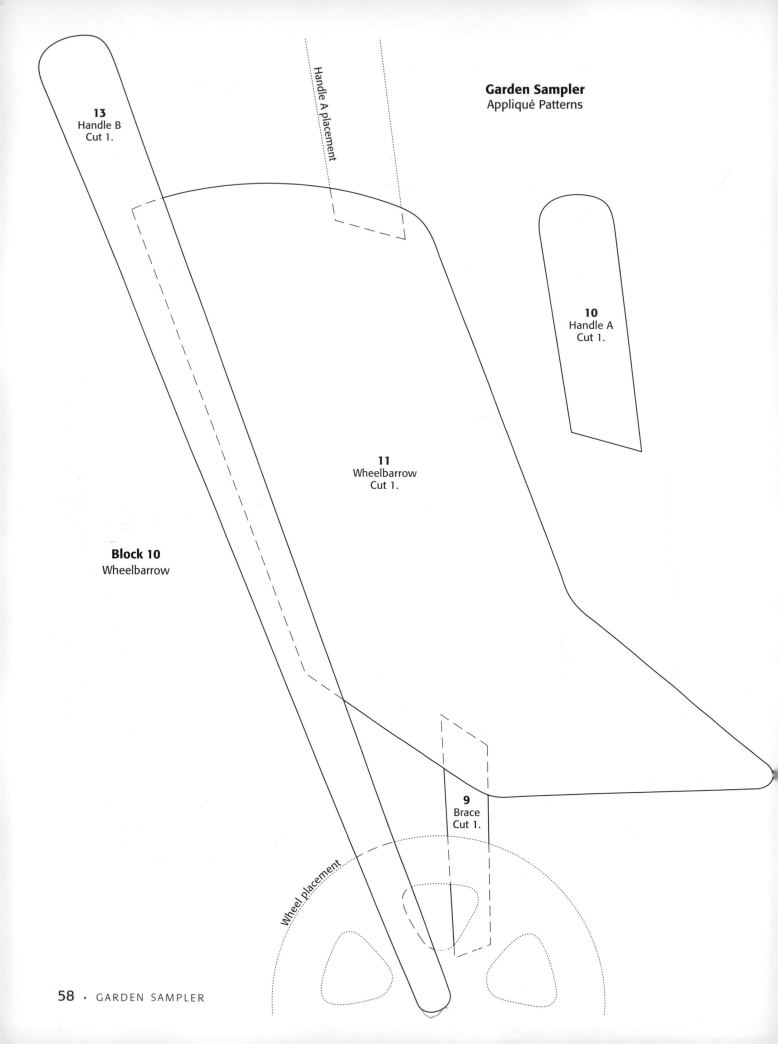

13
Handle B
Cut 1.

Handle A placement

Garden Sampler
Appliqué Patterns

10
Handle A
Cut 1.

11
Wheelbarrow
Cut 1.

Block 10
Wheelbarrow

9
Brace
Cut 1.

Wheel placement

Garland Irish Chain

Garland Irish Chain by Dina Pappas, 2000, Eagle River, Alaska, 88" x 88"; quilted by Marguerite McManus.
Using watercolor fabrics in a traditional Irish Chain pattern creates interlocking garlands.

Finished Watercolor Panel: 70" x 70"
Finished Chain Block: 10" x 10"

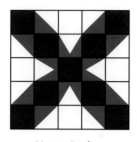

 Background (need 52)   Valley (need 52)

 Large diagonal (need 104)   Full floral (need 117)

Master Design
Make 13.
Use the master design as a guide.
Vary the design as necessary for a realistic look.

Finished Border Chain Block: 10" x 10"

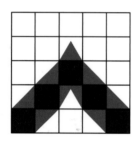

 Background (need 96)

 Large diagonal (need 48)   Tip (need 8)

Valley (need 8)   Full floral (need 40)

Master Design
Make 8.
Use the master design as a guide.
Vary the design as necessary for a realistic look.

Finished Corner Chain Block: 10" x 10"

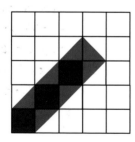

 Background (need 60)

 Large diagonal (need 28)

Full floral (need 12)

Master Design
Make 4.
Use the master design as a guide.
Vary the design as necessary for a realistic look.

Finished Snowball Block: 10" x 10"

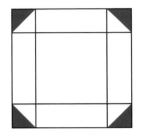

Master Design
Make 12.
Use the master design as a guide.
Vary the design as necessary for a realistic look.

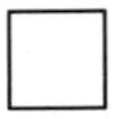

☐ Background (need forty-eight 2½" x 6½" rectangles and twelve 6½" squares)

◪ Large diagonal (need 48)

Finished Border Snowball Block: 10" x 10"

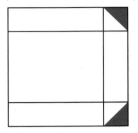

Master Design
Make 12.
Use the master design as a guide.
Vary the design as necessary for a realistic look.

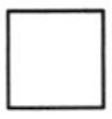

☐ Background (need twenty-four 2½" x 8½" rectangles, twelve 6½" x 8½" rectangles, and twelve 2½" x 6½" rectangles)

◪ Large diagonal (need 24)

CUTTING CHART

Cut all strips across the width of the fabric unless otherwise indicated. Measurements include ¼" seam allowances. Note: If you vary your watercolor panel from the master designs above and on page 60, the pieces needed for each fabric will also vary.

Fabric	Number of Strips	Strip Size	Piece Size	Pieces Needed
Background	2	8½" x 42"	8½" x 6½"	12
	2	6½" x 42"	6½" x 6½"	12
	6	2½" x 42"	2½" x 8½"	24
	10	2½" x 42"	2½" x 6½"	60
	13	2½" x 42"	2½" x 2½"	208
Edge	20	2½" x 42"	2½" x 2½"	320
Full Floral	11	2½" x 42"	2½" x 2½"	169
Inner Border	8	2" x 42"		
Center Border	4	5½" x 86" *		
Binding	5	2½" x 86" *		
Outer Border	10	2½" x 86"		
Backing	3	42" x 90" *		

*Cut from the lengthwise grain of the fabric.

Materials

42"-wide fabric

- 3¼ yds. for background
- 1⅝ yds. edge fabric
- 1 yd. full-floral fabric
- ⅝ yd. for inner border
- 2⅝ yds. for center border and binding
- ⅞ yd. for outer border
- 90" x 90" piece of batting
- 7¾ yds. for backing
- 5⅜ yds. lightweight fusible interfacing, 44" wide

Designing Chain Blocks

1. Cut 2 pieces from the fusible interfacing—one 62½" x 37½" and one 50" x 37½". Using one of the methods outlined in "Preparing Square and Rectangular Panels" on pages 25–26, make one 25 x 15 grid of 2½" squares and one 20 x 15 grid of 2½" squares.

2. Place the larger interfacing grid on your work surface, fusible side up. Following the Chain block design on page 60, place the background pieces for 13 Chain blocks onto the grid.

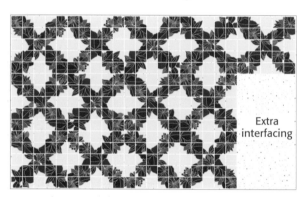

13 Chain blocks

3. Using edge squares, design the outer edges of the garlands. For tips on placing squares, refer to "Placing Edge Pieces" on pages 18–19.

4. Fill in the remaining grid with full-floral squares. To build complete flowers, place squares so the edges echo colors of adjacent squares.

5. Evaluate your design. Make adjustments by replacing or rotating squares as needed. Be prepared to cut a few more squares if necessary.

6. After the watercolor panel is complete, straighten the pieces on the grid. Fuse the squares in place, following the instructions for "Fusing Designs" on page 25.

7. With the small interfacing panel, follow the Border Chain block master design and Corner Chain block master design on page 60 to place the background squares on the interfacing. Make 8 Border Chain blocks and 4 Corner Chain blocks as illustrated. Complete the panel by repeating steps 3–6 (at left).

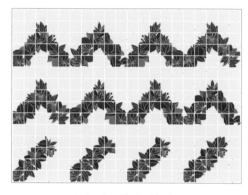

8 Border Chain blocks
and 4 Corner Chain blocks

Designing Snowball Blocks

1. Cut 2 pieces from the fusible interfacing—one 46" x 34½" and one 44" x 34½". Using one of the methods outlined in "Preparing Square and Rectangular Panels" on pages 25–26, make one 4 x 3 grid of 11½" squares and one 4 x 3 grid of 11" x 11½" rectangles.

2. Place the larger interfacing grid on your work surface, fusible side up. Following the Snowball block design on page 61, place the background pieces for 12 Snowball blocks on the interfacing grid.

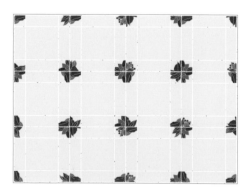

12 Snowball blocks

3. Using edge squares, design the block corners. Turn the darkest corner of the edge fabric toward the outside corners of the block. After the watercolor panel is complete, straighten the pieces on the grid. Fuse the squares in place, following the instructions for "Fusing Designs" on page 25.

4. Place the remaining interfacing grid on your work surface, fusible side up. Following the Border Snowball block master design on page 61, place the background pieces for 12 Border Snowball blocks on the interfacing grid.

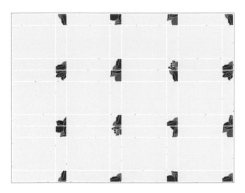

12 Border Snowball blocks

5. Using edge squares, fill in the remaining squares. Turn the darkest corner of the edge squares toward the outside corners on the right side of the block as it is positioned on the interfacing grid. After the watercolor panel is complete, straighten the pieces on the grid. Fuse the squares in place, following the instructions for "Fusing Designs" on page 25.

Stitching

1. Sew the panels together, following the instructions for "Piecing Block Panels" on page 28. Join the long seams first—do not stitch the rows between the blocks. Clip the intersections along each row, but don't separate the blocks yet.

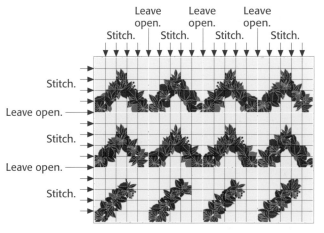

Stitch longest seams first.

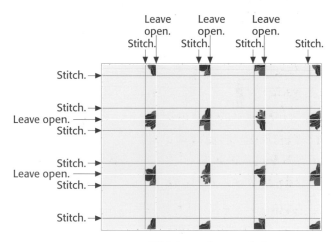

Stitch longest seams first.

2. Stitch the shorter seams, taking care to finger-press the seam allowances in opposite directions. Press well. Cut the blocks apart and square them to 10½" x 10½", following the instructions for "Squaring Panels" on page 28.

3. Refer to the quilt plan below and arrange the watercolor blocks to form the pattern. Join the blocks to form rows. Join the rows, matching seams and easing as necessary.

Adding Borders

1. Join the 2" inner border strips, and then cut into four 76" strips. Join the 2½" outer border strips, and then cut into four 86" strips. Join a 2" inner border strip, a 5½" center border strip, and a 2½" outer border strip for each side of the quilt top as shown, matching centers.

2. Sew the pieced border strips to the quilt top, following the directions for "Mitered Borders" on pages 86–87.

Quilting Suggestions and Finishing

NOTE: *For general quilting instructions and help with specific techniques, refer to "Finishing Techniques" on pages 88–95.*

1. Piece the backing fabric and trim to 90" x 90". Layer the backing, batting, and quilt top. Pin-baste the quilt sandwich.

2. If you want to follow my quilting plan, use free-motion quilting to quilt a pattern within each diamond and in each side triangle. Stipple-quilt the remaining background areas. Meander-quilt through the floral areas, stitching around individual flowers. Quilt borders as desired.

3. Referring to "Binding" on pages 93–95, join the binding strips and sew them to the quilt top.

Quilt Plan

Celtic Garden Maze

Celtic Garden Maze by Dina Pappas, 2000, Tecumseh, Michigan, 62" x 62".
Some of the same blocks used in "Garland Irish Chain" on page 59 were arranged in a new setting here.
The background areas created by the new arrangement are the perfect place for appliquéd flowers.

Finished Watercolor Panel: 50" x 50"
Finished Chain Block: 10" x 10"

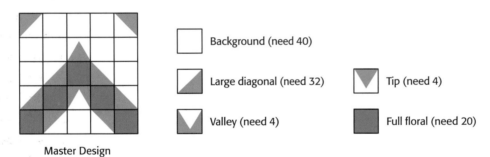

Master Design
Make 8.
Use the master design as a guide.
Vary the design as necessary for a realistic look.

Background (need 32)   Valley (need 32)

Large diagonal (need 64)   Full floral (need 72)

Finished Celtic Border Block: 10" x 10"

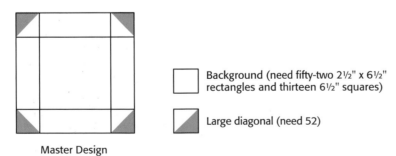

Master Design
Make 4.
Use the master design as a guide.
Vary the design as necessary for a realistic look.

Background (need 40)

Large diagonal (need 32)   Tip (need 4)

Valley (need 4)   Full floral (need 20)

Finished Snowball Block: 10" x 10"

Master Design
Make 13.
Use the master design as a guide.
Vary the design as necessary for a realistic look.

Background (need fifty-two 2½" x 6½"
rectangles and thirteen 6½" squares)

Large diagonal (need 52)

Cutting Chart

Cut all strips across the width of the fabric unless otherwise indicated. Measurements include ¼" seam allowances. Note: If you vary your watercolor panel from the master designs on page 66, the pieces needed for each fabric will also vary.

Fabric	Number of Strips	Strip Size	Piece Size	Pieces Needed
Background	2	6½" x 42"	6½" x 6½"	13
	4	6½" x 42"	2½" x 6½"	52
	5	2½" x 42"	2½" x 2½"	72
Edge	12	2½" x 42"	2½" x 2½"	188
Full Floral	6	2½" x 42"	2½" x 2½"	92
Inner Border	6	2" x 42"		
Outer Border	7	5" x 42"		
Binding	7	2½" x 42"		
Backing	2	42" x 66"*		

*Cut from the lengthwise grain of the fabric.

Materials

42"-wide fabric

- 1⅝ yds. for background
- 1 yd. edge fabric
- ⅝ yd. full-floral fabric
- ⅜ yd. total assorted green fabrics for leaf and stem appliqués
- ¼ yd. total assorted pink fabrics for appliqués (7" dark pink and 2" medium pink)
- ¼ yd. total assorted blue fabrics for appliqués (3" blue-purple and 2" aqua)
- ½ yd. for inner border
- 1¼ yds. for outer border
- ⅝ yd. for binding
- 66" x 66" piece of batting
- 3⅞ yds. for backing
- 3⅛ yds. lightweight fusible interfacing, 44" wide
- Freezer paper

Designing Chain Blocks

1. Cut a piece of fusible interfacing 50" x 37½". Using one of the methods outlined in "Preparing Grids" on page 22, make a 20 x 15 grid of 2½" squares.

2. Place the interfacing grid on your work surface, fusible side up. Following the Chain block design and the Celtic Border block design on page 66, place the background pieces on the interfacing grid. Make 8 Chain blocks and 4 Celtic Border blocks as illustrated.

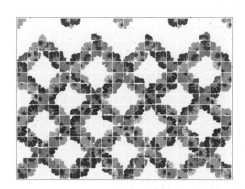

4 Celtic Border blocks and 8 Chain blocks

3. Using edge squares, design the outer edges of the garlands. For tips on placing squares, refer to "Placing Edge Pieces" on pages 18–19.

4. Fill in the remaining grid with full-floral squares. To build complete flowers, place squares so edges echo the colors of adjacent squares.

5. Evaluate your design. Make adjustments by replacing or rotating squares as needed. Be prepared to cut a few more squares if necessary.

6. After the watercolor panel is complete, straighten the pieces on the grid. Fuse the squares in place, following the instructions for "Fusing Designs" on page 25.

Designing Snowball Blocks

1. Cut a piece of fusible interfacing 57½" x 34½". Using one of the methods outlined in "Preparing Square and Rectangular Panels" on pages 25–26, make one 5 x 3 grid of 11½" squares.

2. Place the interfacing grid on your work surface, fusible side up. Following the Snowball block design on page 66, place the background pieces on the interfacing grid. Make 13 Snowball blocks as illustrated.

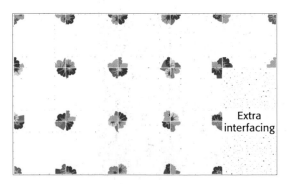

13 Snowball blocks

3. Using edge squares, design the block corners. Turn the darkest corner of the edge fabric toward the outside corners of the block. After the watercolor panel is complete, straighten the pieces on the grid. Fuse the squares in place, following the instructions for "Fusing Designs" on page 25.

Stitching

1. Sew the panels together, following the instructions for "Piecing Block Panels" on page 28. Join the long seams first—do not stitch the rows between the blocks. Clip the intersections along each row, but don't separate the blocks yet.

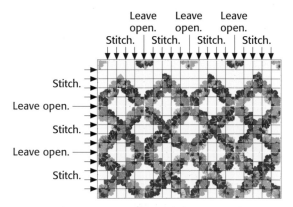

Stitch longest seams first.

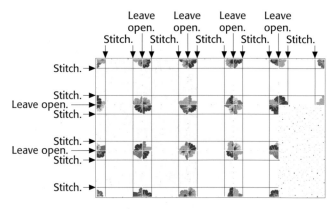

Stitch longest seams first.

2. Stitch the shorter seams, taking care to finger-press the seam allowances in opposite directions. Press well. Cut the blocks apart and square them to 10½" x 10½", following the instructions for "Squaring Panels" on page 28.

3. Arrange the watercolor blocks to form the pattern as shown in the quilt plan on page 69. Rotate and swap blocks to form the strongest arrangement. Mark the center block and place a pin in the corner of each remaining Snowball block to indicate the base for the outside appliqués.

Appliqué

1. Following steps 1–4 in "Freezer-Paper Appliqué" on page 83, trace the appliqué template patterns on pages 70–71 onto freezer paper and prepare appliqué pieces for 1 Center block and 12 Snowball blocks.

2. Join the pieces to form flower units as shown. Arrange the flower units on the blocks as shown. Continue as described in steps 5 and 6 in "Freezer-Paper Appliqué" on pages 83–84.

Quilt Assembly and Finishing

NOTE: *For general quilting instructions and help with specific techniques, refer to "Finishing Techniques" on pages 88–95.*

1. Join the blocks to form rows. Join the rows, matching seams and easing as necessary.

2. Join 2" inner border strips. Add the borders to the quilt top, following the instructions for "Straight-Cut Borders" on pages 85–86. Repeat for the 5" outer border strips.

3. Piece the backing fabric to 66" x 66". Layer the backing, batting, and quilt top. Pin-baste the quilt sandwich.

4. If you want to follow my quilting plan, proceed as follows: Stipple-quilt the background areas and meander-quilt through the floral areas, stitching around individual flowers to highlight blooms. Add detail quilting to the appliqués to add veins to the leaves and flowers.

5. Referring to "Binding" on pages 93–95, join the binding strips and sew them to the quilt top.

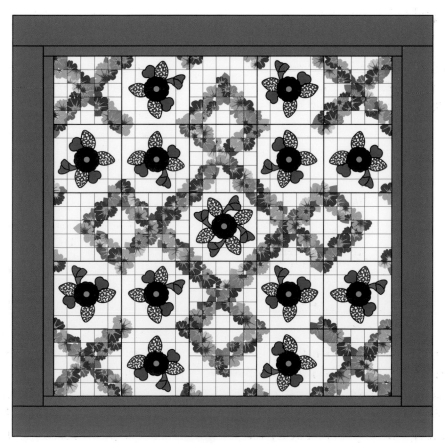

Quilt Plan

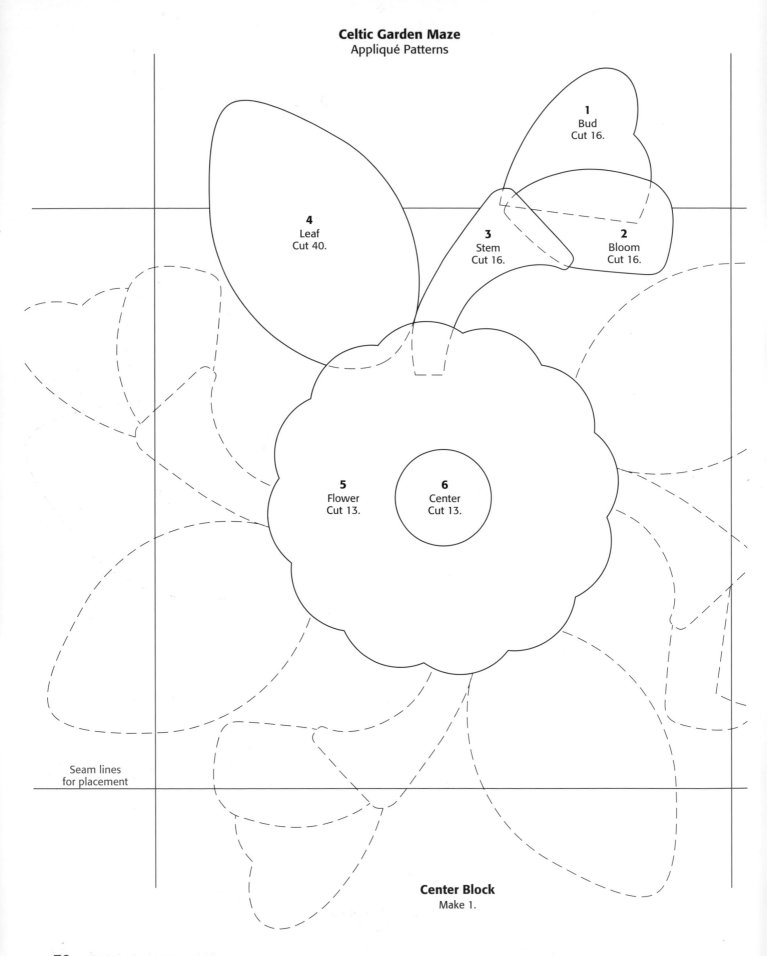

Celtic Garden Maze
Appliqué Patterns

1
Bud
Cut 16.

4
Leaf
Cut 40.

3
Stem
Cut 16.

2
Bloom
Cut 16.

5
Flower
Cut 13.

6
Center
Cut 13.

Seam lines
for placement

Center Block
Make 1.

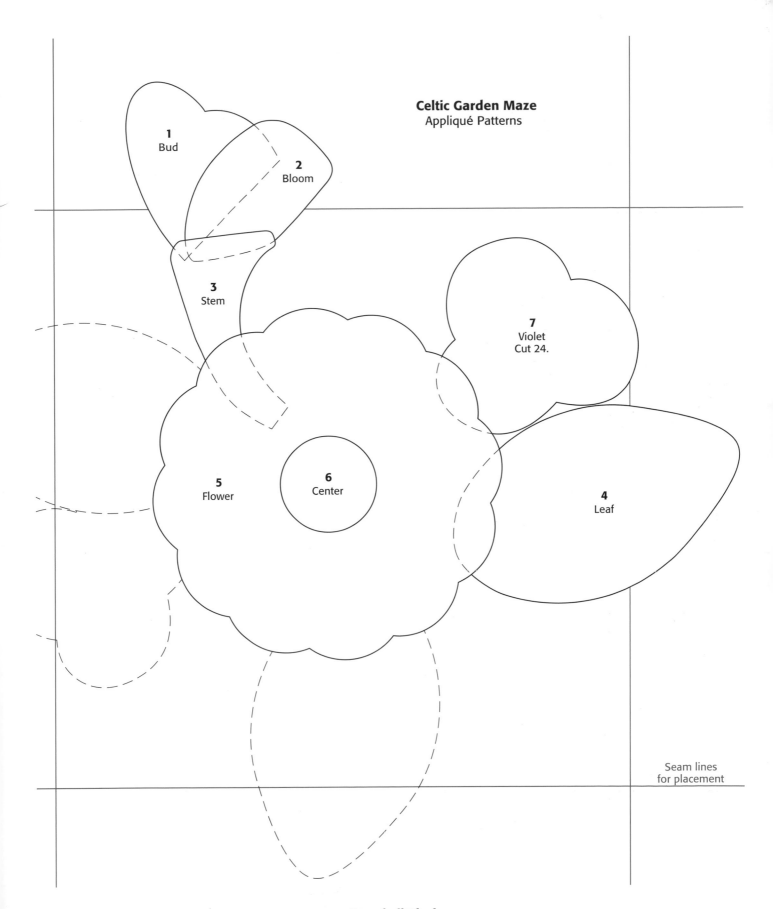

Celtic Garden Maze
Appliqué Patterns

1
Bud

2
Bloom

3
Stem

7
Violet
Cut 24.

5
Flower

6
Center

4
Leaf

Seam lines
for placement

Snowball Block
Make 12.

Four Vintage Baskets

Four Vintage Baskets by Dina Pappas, 2000, Tecumseh, Michigan, 30⅜" x 33¾".
A vintage border fabric was used to create the flowers in this traditional-looking quilt. Another color of the floral fabric was used in the border to make a garland frame. The quilt was constructed from triangle pieces.

Finished Watercolor Panel: 14⅞" x 18¼"
Triangle Size: 3½" equilateral

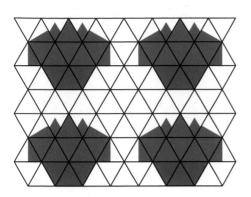

 Background (need 45)

 Large diagonal (need 16)

 Tip (need 8)

 Full floral (need 24)

 Basket (need 12)

Master Design
Use the master design as a guide.
Vary the design as necessary for a realistic look.

CUTTING CHART

Cut all strips across the width of the fabric unless otherwise indicated. Measurements include ¼" seam allowances. Note: If you vary your watercolor panel from the master design above, the pieces needed for each fabric will also vary.

Fabric	Number of Strips	Strip Size	Triangle Size*	Pieces Needed
Background	3	3" x 42"	3½" equilateral	45
	2	2" x 22"		
	2	2" x 25"		
Edge	2	3" x 42"	3½" equilateral	24
Full Floral	2	3" x 42"	3½" equilateral	
Basket	1	3" x 42"	3½" equilateral	
Center Border	2	2" x 25"		
	2	2" x 28"		
Outer Border	2	5¼" x 30"		
	2	5¼" x 33"		
Binding	4	2½"		

*3½ equilateral triangles measure 3" high from center of triangle base to point.

Materials

42"-wide fabric

- ½ yd. for background fabric and inner border
- ¼ yd. edge fabric
- ¼ yd. full-floral fabric
- ½ yd. for baskets and center border
- ¾ yd. for outer border
- ⅜ yd. for binding
- 35" x 38" piece of batting
- 1 yd. for backing
- ¾ yd. lightweight fusible interfacing, 22" wide**

** Purchase wider gridded interfacing if desired, but the extra width isn't needed for this project.

Designing

1. Cut the fusible interfacing to 21" x 24½". See "Preparing Triangle Grids" on page 00 and make a 7 x 8 triangle grid with 3" intervals, beginning with horizontal lines, as illustrated. A triangle grid with lines drawn 3" apart yields 3½" equilateral triangles that measure 3" from the center of each triangle base to the point.

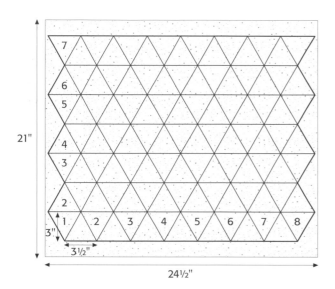

2. Place the interfacing grid on your work surface, fusible side up. Following the Four Baskets master design on page 73, place the basket and background pieces on the interfacing grid.

3. Using edge triangles, create the outer edge of each bouquet. Place the triangles on the grid with the floral portion turned toward the bouquet.

4. Fill in the remaining grid with full-floral triangles. To build complete flowers, place triangles so the edges echo the colors of adjacent pieces.

5. Evaluate your design. Make adjustments by replacing or rotating pieces as needed. Be prepared to cut a few more triangles if necessary.

6. After the watercolor panel is complete, straighten the pieces on the grid. Fuse the triangles in place following the instructions for "Fusing Designs" on page 25.

Stitching

1. Sew the panel together, following the instructions for "Piecing Triangle Panels" on pages 26–28. Press well.

2. Square the finished panels to 14⅞" x 18¼", following the instructions for "Squaring Panels" on page 28 and leaving ¼"-wide seam allowances on the sides.

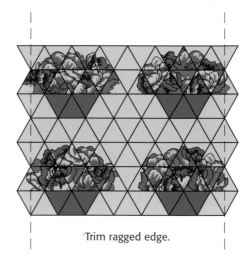

Trim ragged edge.

Adding Borders

1. Join a 2" x 22" background strip, a 2" x 25" center border strip, and a 5¼" x 30" outer border strip as shown, matching centers. Make 2 of these border strips. Referring to "Mitered Borders" on page 86, stitch strips to the sides of the quilt.

2. Join the remaining background, center, and outer border strips to make 2 more border strips. Stitch them to the top and bottom of the quilt, mitering the corners.

Quilting Suggestions and Finishing

NOTE: *For general quilting instructions and help with specific techniques, refer to "Finishing Techniques" on pages 88–95.*

1. Trim the backing fabric to 35" x 38". Layer the backing, batting, and quilt top. Pin-baste the quilt sandwich.

2. If you want to follow my quilting plan, proceed as follows: Stipple-quilt the background areas and meander-quilt through the floral areas, stitching around individual flowers to highlight blooms. Quilt the borders as desired.

3. Referring to "Binding" on pages 93–95, join the binding strips and sew them to the quilt top.

Quilt Plan

Watercolor Nosegays

Watercolor Nosegays by Dina Pappas, 2000, Eagle River, Alaska, 42" x 52½".
The combinations are endless when fussy cutting floral fabrics. The kaleidoscope effect
adds an interesting element to this quilt of triangles framed by a built-in ribbon.

Finished Watercolor Panel: 34" x 44½"
Triangle Size: 3½" equilateral

Master Design
Use the master design as a guide.
Vary the design as necessary for a realistic look.

 Background (need 144)

 Ribbon border (need 44)

 Ribbon border (need 96)

 Full-floral 1 (need 72 "fussy cut")

 Full-floral 2 (need 72 "fussy cut")

Full-floral 3 (need 126 "fussy cut")

Materials

42"-wide fabric

- 1⅜ yds. for background and border
- ⅝ yd. edge fabric **
- ¾ yd. full-floral fabric **
- ⅜ yd. dark fabric for ribbon
- ⅝ yd. medium fabric for ribbon
- ½ yd. for binding
- 46" x 57" piece of batting
- 2¾ yds. for backing
- 2¾ yds. lightweight fusible interfacing, 44" wide

** This yardage is for triangles that are not fussy cut. For triangles that are fussy cut, allow additional fabric for 6 repeats, which will vary depending on the fabric design.

CUTTING CHART

Cut all strips across the width of the fabric unless otherwise indicated. Measurements include ¼" seam allowances. Note: If you vary your watercolor panel from the master design on page 77, the pieces needed for each fabric will also vary.

Fabric	Number of Strips	Strip Size	Triangle Size*	Pieces Needed
Background	7	3" x 42"	3½" equilateral	144
	5	4½" x 42"		
Edge	6	3" x 42"	3½" equilateral	126 **
Full Floral	7	3" x 42"	3½" equilateral	144 **
Dark Ribbon	3	3" x 42"	3½" equilateral	44
Medium Ribbon	5	3" x 42"	3½" equilateral	102
Binding	5	2½" x 42"		
Backing	2	42" x 46" ***		

*3½" equilateral triangles measure 3" high from center of the triangle base to the point.
**See "Fussy Cutting" below to fussy-cut the edge and full-floral triangles for this project.
***Cut from the lengthwise grain of the fabric.

Fussy Cutting

1. To fussy-cut fabric for this project and achieve a kaleidoscope effect, locate the repeating pattern in your edge and full-floral fabrics. From both fabrics cut 6 rectangles, each 9" x 17" or larger, of the repeating floral pattern. Layer the repeating motifs and position pins through the common points in each layer. Smooth and pin the layers together.

2. For the full-floral triangles, cut the stack of six 9" x 17" full-floral rectangles from step 1 into 3 stacks of strips measuring 3" x 17". Cut the stacks of strips into 24 sets of 6 equilateral triangles. Pin each set of triangles together.

3. For the edge triangles, cut the stack of six 9" x 17" edge-fabric rectangles from step 1 into 3 stacks of strips measuring 3" x 17". Cut the stacks of strips into 24 sets of 6 equilateral triangles. From the 24 sets of 6 equilateral triangles, you will need 6 sets of 6 triangles and 18 sets of 5 triangles. One edge-fabric triangle in each of 18 sets will not be used for this project. Pin each set of triangles together.

Repeat

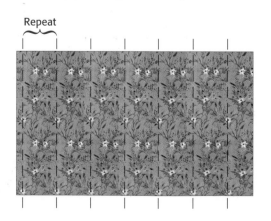

Designing

1. Cut the fusible interfacing into two 48" pieces and join the pieces along a 48" edge as in "Joining Interfacing Panels" on page 23. Trim interfacing to 48" x 63". See "Equilateral Triangle Grids" on page 22, and make a 16 x 18 triangle grid with 3" intervals, beginning with vertical lines, as illustrated. A triangle grid with lines drawn 3" apart yields 3½" equilateral triangles, which measure 3" from the center of each triangle base to the point.

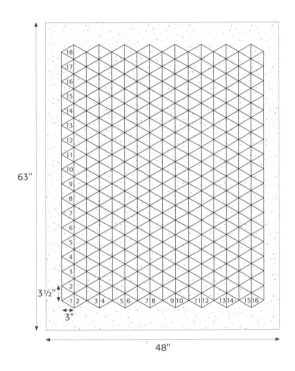

2. Place the interfacing grid on your work surface, fusible side up. Following the Watercolor Nosegays master design on page 77, place the dark and medium ribbon and background pieces on the interfacing grid.

3. Fill in the grid with full-floral triangles. Build 6-pointed stars, placing triangles so the edges echo the colors of adjacent pieces. If using fussy-cut triangles, use 1 set for the center hexagon and 1 set for the points of each nosegay.

4. Using edge triangles, soften the edges of the 6-pointed stars by rotating pieces so sides echo colors of adjacent pieces. If using fussy-cut triangles, use 2 sets of 6 around each star in the top row and 2 sets of 5 around each remaining star.

5. Evaluate your design. Make adjustments by replacing or rotating triangles as needed. Be prepared to cut a few more triangles if necessary.

6. After the watercolor panel is complete, straighten the pieces on the grid. Fuse the triangles in place, following the instructions for "Fusing Designs" on page 25.

Stitching

1. Sew the panel together, following the instructions for "Piecing Triangle Panels" on pages 26–28. Press well.

2. Square the finished panels to 34" x 44½", following the instructions for "Squaring Panels" on page 28 and leaving ¼" seam allowances on the sides.

3. Join three 4½" background strips for the border and add borders referring to the instructions for "Straight-Cut Borders" on pages 85–86.

Quilting Suggestions and Finishing

NOTE: *For general quilting instructions and help with specific techniques, refer to "Finishing Techniques" on pages 88–95.*

1. Trim the backing fabric to 46" x 57". Layer the backing, batting, and quilt top. Pin-baste the quilt sandwich.

2. If you want to follow my quilting plan, proceed as follows: Stipple-quilt the background areas and meander-quilt through the floral areas, stitching around individual flowers to highlight blooms. Quilt borders as desired.

3. Referring to "Binding" on pages 93–95, join the binding strips and sew them to the quilt top.

Quilt Plan

Quiltmaking Techniques

Rotary Cutting

A ROTARY cutter, ruler, and self-healing cutting mat allow you to cut a large number of pieces quickly and accurately. For safety, close your blade after each cut. Cut away from you and change the blade regularly.

Cutting Strips, Squares, and Rectangles

1. Fold the fabric in half with selvages matching and the fold next to you. Align one edge of a square ruler on the edge of the fold. Position a long ruler up against the square at an exact right angle to the fold. Remove the square ruler and cut along the edge of the long ruler.

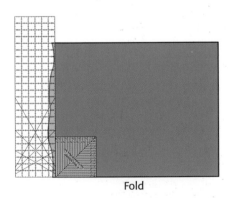

Fold

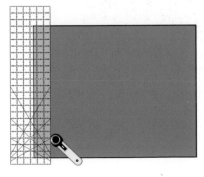

2. Using the long ruler, cut the strips of the required width. Keep firm pressure on the ruler as you cut. To prevent the ruler from shifting, walk your hand, thumb to fingers, up the ruler. Cut up to the level of your fingertips, stop, shift your hand, and continue.

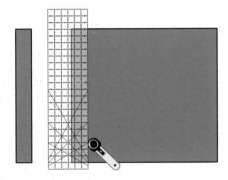

3. Crosscut the strips into squares or rectangles. To save time, layer strips as you cut.

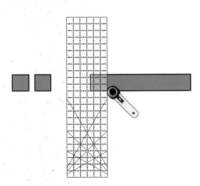

Cutting Equilateral Triangles

Equilateral triangles are triangles that measure the same length on each side. The angle at each corner is 60 degrees. Equilateral strips can be rotary cut from straight-grain strips using your ruler.

1. Cut strips to the required width. The width of the strips is equal to the height of the triangle, measured from the center of the base to the point directly across from the base. To save time, layer strips as you cut.

2. Align the 60-degree line of the ruler with the top edge of the strip. Cut from raw edge to raw edge.

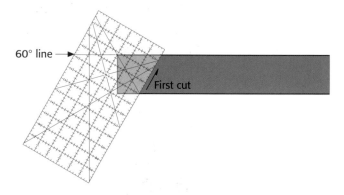

3. Rotate the ruler to align the two 60-degree lines on the ruler with the point of the triangle. Cut from raw edge to raw edge.

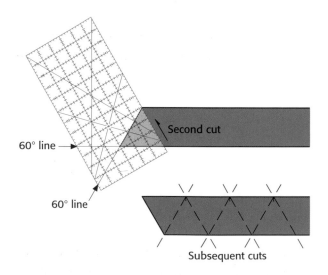

Machine Piecing

IT IS necessary to use an exact ¼"-wide seam allowance in quiltmaking. Small variations can distort a quilt, especially when joining many pieces. To set up your machine for an accurate ¼" seam allowance, use one of the following methods:

- If your machine can make a zigzag stitch, adjust the needle position so that the needle comes down exactly ¼" from the edge of the presser foot. Use a scrap of graph paper with ¼" grid lines as a guide.

- Make a fabric guide by laying a strip of masking tape or moleskin on the needle plate ¼" away from the needle. Moleskin, available in drugstores, creates a ridge to help guide the fabric.

- Purchase a quilter's presser foot that measures exactly ¼" from the center needle position to the right edge of the foot.

Using a fresh needle at the beginning of each quilting project keeps burrs and dull needles from damaging your quilt. It's especially important to use fresh needles when machine quilting.

Clean and oil your sewing machine as often as manufacturer's instructions suggest. A can of compressed air, available at office-supply stores, cleans out lint that accumulates on the machine and in the bobbin area. Your sewing machine will run better and sound better with a bit of tender loving care.

The manual is an excellent reference tool that will help you keep your machine friendly and happy. It may introduce you to dials and knobs you never noticed before. A sewing-machine repair center or dealer may be another good source of help. Let them know what you want to do, and they may be able to provide instruction or find the attachment that will make your piecing easier.

Appliqué Techniques

APPLIQUÉ IS used on "Two-Colored Blooming Hedges" on page 34, "Garden Sampler" on page 51, and "Celtic Garden Maze" on page 65. There are many ways to appliqué, and I will touch on just a few of those methods here.

Needle-Turn Appliqué

Needle-turn appliqué is wonderful because you can take it with you to a waiting room or to meetings.

1. Mark the appliqué shape on the right side of the fabric.

2. Cut out the shape a scant ¼" beyond the marked line. Clip the seam allowances on inner corners and inside curves.

3. Pin or baste the shape to the background.

4. Use the tip of a needle to turn a bit of the seam allowance under and hold it down with your thumb. Blindstitch the turned-under edge to the background. Before you get to the end of the turned seam allowance, turn under a bit more and continue your stitching. For sharp points and outside corners, stitch all the way to the tip of the point before turning under the seam allowance on the adjacent side. If the edge of one appliqué piece will be covered with another, it's not necessary to turn under the edge.

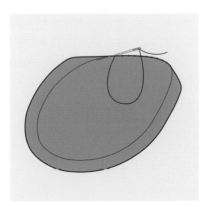

Freezer-Paper Appliqué

Freezer-paper appliqué is faster than needle-turn appliqué. Make either small hidden stitches or decorative ones, by hand or machine, to secure the appliqué to the background.

1. Trace reversed appliqué shapes onto the unwaxed side of the freezer paper and cut out the shape exactly on the traced line.

2. With shiny side down, place the freezer paper template on the wrong side of the fabric. Leave ¾" between pieces for seam allowances. Fuse the templates to the fabric using a hot, dry iron.

3. Cut out each piece, leaving ¼" seam allowances. Clip inner curves and inner corners and trim outer corners and seam allowance to $3/16$".

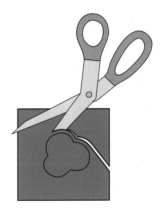

4. Apply water-soluble glue stick to the wrong side of the seam allowances and press them against the freezer paper.

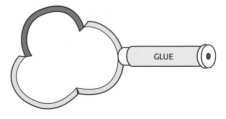

5. Position the appliqué design on the background. Stitch in place, using one of the appliqué stitches on page 84.

6. Cut away the fabric behind the appliqué piece, leaving a ¼"-wide seam allowance. Spray with a light mist of water to dissolve the glue. Remove the freezer paper and press.

Appliqué Stitches

There are many ways to secure appliqué pieces to the background. Whether you prefer hand stitching or machine stitching, blind or decorative stitches, there's a method to create the look you desire.

Hand Appliqué Stitch

1. Starting with a single strand of thread about 18" long, thread the needle and tie a knot in one end. Use needles called Sharps. They are longer and thinner than quilting needles and make fine stitches.

2. Bring the needle up through the background and the folded edge of the appliqué piece.

3. Take the first stitch by moving your needle straight off the appliqué and inserting it into the background fabric. If you are right-handed, stitch from right to left. If you are left-handed, stitch from left to right.

4. Guide the needle under the background fabric, parallel to the edge of the appliqué, and bring it up about ⅛" away. As you bring the needle back up, catch only 2 or 3 threads of the appliqué.

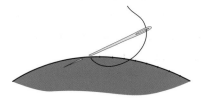

5. Take the next stitch by moving the needle straight off the appliqué edge and into the background fabric. Keep the stitch length consistent as you continue around the piece.

6. To end your stitching, pull the needle to the wrong side. Take 2 small stitches behind the appliqué piece, making knots by bringing your needle through the loops. Clip off the excess thread.

Machine Appliqué Stitches

Machine appliqué is my preferred method because I get nice results in less time than it would take if I worked by hand. When machine stitching appliqués, decrease the top tension and use transparent thread in the top thread of the machine and fine machine embroidery thread in the bobbin. Use a small machine needle for less noticeable stitches and an open-toe appliqué foot to help you see the stitching.

If you can adjust the length and width of your sewing machine's blind hemstitch, you can quickly appliqué pieces in place. Practice adjusting the machine, then note the settings. I keep my notes taped to my machine for quick reference. Both fusible and freezer-paper appliqué are well suited to machine blind stitching.

1. Set your sewing machine for a short blind stitch. The machine will take 4 to 7 straight stitches along the edge of the appliqué piece, then swing over. Adjust the width of the stitch so it catches 2 to 3 threads of the appliqué. Adjust the length so there is about ⅛" between the wide swings. Make adjustments to the best of your machine's ability and take notes.

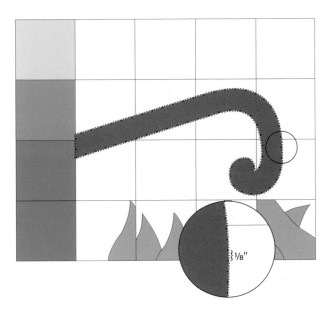

2. Position the appliqués on the background fabric, starting with the bottom layers and building up.

3. Position the needle in the background fabric so that it just touches the piece to be sewn. Blind-stitch around the piece—the straight stitches will be made in the ditch and the sideways stitch will catch the edge.

Adding Borders

IT IS best to choose your border fabrics after your center panel is completed. To add color to watercolor quilts without overpowering the design, you may wish to choose a tone-on-tone fabric for your border. A safe option is to choose two colors from the watercolor design for the inner and outer borders, or you can use light and dark versions of a single color.

Position the watercolor panel up against possible border fabrics. Step back and see what works. Consider the finished border widths as you layer the fabrics you are auditioning. Check fabrics in both the inner and outer border positions to see what you like best. Because there are so many choices, I enjoy making the same watercolor design more than once to see how different borders change the look and highlight different colors.

Straight-Cut Borders

1. Measure the quilt top vertically at the center from raw edge to raw edge. Cut 2 border strips to that measurement. Mark the centers of the border strips and the centers along the sides of the quilt top. Join the border strips to the sides of the quilt, matching ends and centers and easing if necessary. Press the seam allowances toward the borders.

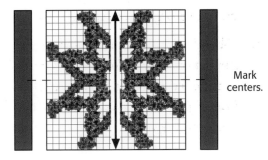

Mark centers.

Measure length at center.

2. Measure the quilt top horizontally at the center from raw edge to raw edge, including the border pieces just added. Cut 2 border strips to that measurement. Mark the centers of the border strips and the centers of the top and bottom of

the quilt top. Join the border strips to the top and bottom of the quilt, matching ends and centers and easing if necessary. Press the seam allowances toward the borders.

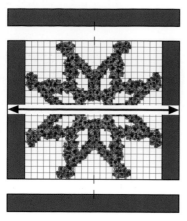

Measure width at center.

Borders with Corner Squares

1. Measure the quilt top vertically at the center from raw edge to raw edge. Cut 2 border strips to that measurement. Measure the quilt top horizontally at the center from raw edge to raw edge. Cut 2 border strips to that measurement.

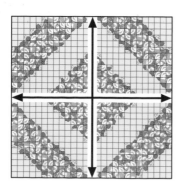

2. Cut or piece corner squares the same width as the borders, including seam allowances.

3. Join the side border strips to the quilt top. Press seams toward the borders.

4. Join a corner square to each end of the top and bottom strips. Press seams toward the border strips. Then join the strips to the top and bottom of the quilt.

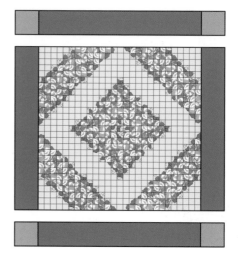

Mitered Borders

1. Estimate the finished outside dimensions of your quilt including borders. Cut 4 border strips to that length plus 2" to 3". If your quilt is to have multiple borders, join the individual border strips along the lengthwise edges with center points matching and treat the resulting unit as a single border.

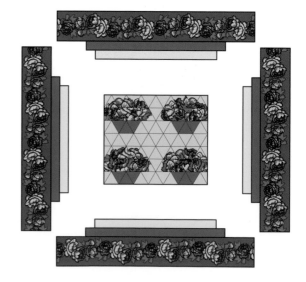

2. Mark ¼" seam intersections on all 4 corners of the quilt top. Mark the center of each side.

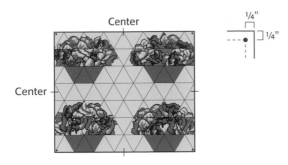

3. Mark the center of each border strip. Measure the distance between the corner marks at the top and bottom of the quilt top and mark the measured distance on the inner edges of 2 border strips, keeping the center mark at the center. Repeat for the sides.

4. With right sides together, lay the border strip on the quilt top, matching the center and corner marks. Stitch from corner mark to corner mark and no farther. Do not backstitch in case you need to remove a stitch or two. The stitching lines must meet exactly at the corners. Repeat with the remaining border strips.

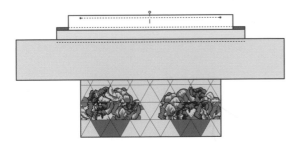

5. With right sides together, fold the quilt diagonally so the border strips are aligned. Using a right angle or quilter's ruler marked with a 45-degree angle, draw a line on the wrong side of the top border strip, from the corner mark to the outer edge as shown.

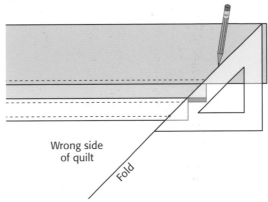

6. Secure the borders with pins and stitch on the drawn line. Make sure the seam is flat and accurate, then trim the seam allowances to ¼". Press open. Repeat at remaining corners.

Finishing Techniques

Preparing to Quilt

Marking the Quilting Design

Quilting patterns are as varied as patchwork patterns. You can mark quilting designs either before or after you put the layers together. For channel, stipple, and in-the-ditch quilting, you don't need to mark the quilt top at all.

To mark before the layers are put together:

Use a sharp No. 2 pencil or quilt marking tool and mark lightly. Test your marking tools on scraps from your project first to make sure marks can be removed. Long rulers are helpful in drawing straight-line grids. To transfer designs, either cut quilting-pattern templates or stencils from plastic or cardboard and draw around them, or place a drawn pattern and the quilt top on a light box or window and trace.

To mark after the layers are put together:

Use chalk or masking tape to mark quilting designs right before you stitch. Do not leave masking tape on the quilt top any longer than necessary because it can leave marks.

Preparing the Quilt Sandwich

LAYERING THE quilt top with batting and backing makes the quilt "sandwich." You need to baste these layers together before you quilt.

Backing fabric of a solid color will accent the quilting. A small-scale print with several colors will help hide the quilting stitches and allow you to blend several colors of quilting thread. Beginning machine quilters may like the way a print forgives a few errors.

In this book, yardage requirements for backings are based on 44"-wide fabric. Backings for quilts that finish wider than 40" must be pieced. If you prefer unpieced backings, purchase 60"- or 90"-wide fabric.

In general, cut or assemble a quilt backing that is at least 2" larger than your quilt top on all sides. For smaller quilts, you may be able to get by with less. On pieced backings, press seams open to make quilting easier.

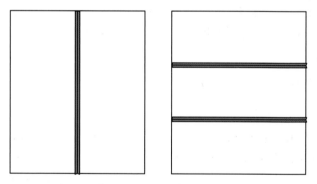

For a large quilt, you may need to piece the backing.

To assemble the quilt sandwich, spread the quilt backing on the floor or on a large table, right side down. Cover it with batting, then center the quilt top on the batting. Smooth the top so it lies flat.

Basting

For Hand Quilting

1. Starting in the center, make diagonal, vertical, and horizontal rows of basting stitches about 6" to 8" apart.

2. Place the quilt in a hoop or frame, making sure the layers are smooth and free of wrinkles.

3. Remove the basting stitches when quilting is complete.

For Machine Quilting

Basting threads catch on the presser foot and are difficult to remove so pin-baste when you plan to machine quilt. Start in the center and pin the layers with size 2 rustproof safety pins, but do not close the pins at this stage. After you have completely pinned the quilt, check that there are no wrinkles on the back, then close the safety pins.

Set up your sewing machine with plenty of clear table space beside and behind it. If the quilt is large, it will have to be rolled or folded neatly to fit under the machine. Attach a walking foot and quilt major sections of the quilt in the ditch (see section at right, below). Once the quilt is anchored and divided into manageable sections, you can add detail quilting.

Remove the pins from each section before you begin to quilt. This way, you won't have to interrupt your quilting rhythm to remove pins in the way.

Quilting

Hand Quilting

Even if you piece with interfacing you can still hand quilt. Lightweight interfacing adds minimal bulk and won't interfere with the beautiful look of handmade stitches.

Pulling the needle through the seam allowances can be difficult, so plan your quilting design to avoid areas where pieces intersect. Use a quilting thread and a Between needle in a size you find comfortable. At the beginning of a quilting session, thread several needles with 18" lengths of thread so you won't have to frequently stop and re-thread.

1. Begin quilting with a knotted thread. Insert the needle through the top layer of the quilt about 1" from the point where you want to start stitching.

Slide the needle through the batting and bring the needle out at the starting point. Gently tug on the thread until the knot pops through the fabric and is buried in the batting.

2. Take a backstitch and begin quilting. Insert the needle vertically until it touches the finger beneath the quilt, then rock it upward to make a small stitch. Repeat for several stitches before pulling the thread through. Use a thimble to protect the finger pushing the needle through. Consider wearing a rubber fingertip on your index finger to help you grip the needle.

3. To end your stitches, make a single knot about ¼" from the quilt top. Take one backstitch into the quilt and tug on the knot until it pops into the batting. Bring the needle out ¾" away from your last stitch and clip the thread.

Machine Quilting

Straight-Line Quilting

Use straight-line quilting to make simple lines and secure quilt layers together. On large quilts, use straight-line quilting to anchor the sandwich and break the quilt into manageable sections.

Quilting in the Ditch

A ditch is formed along a seam when seam allowances are pressed to one side, creating a ridge. One side of the seam will have three layers of fabric, the other a single layer. When quilting in the ditch, the needle should be on the single layer, nestled close to the ridge made by the seam allowance. Good ditch quilting will disappear into the seam. Press the seam allowances carefully as you piece so you will have a straight ditch to stitch in.

Use thread that matches the fabric, transparent nylon thread, or a neutral color that blends if you'll be quilting over multiple fabrics.

1. Attach a walking foot. This special foot will evenly feed the 3 layers of the quilt sandwich through the machine.

2. Set stitch length to 8 to 12 stitches per inch.

3. Pull the bobbin thread to the top of the quilt sandwich and lock the threads. Holding the top thread firmly, take 1 stitch. Tug gently on the top thread and draw the bobbin thread up through the sandwich. Hold both tails firmly, and take 4 tiny stitches to anchor the stitching and prevent tangled threads on the back.

4. Keeping your eye on the needle, stitch along the edge of the seam without crossing to the other side.

Channel Quilting

Channel quilting is simply straight, parallel lines of quilting. This style of quilting works well on sashing and borders, and on printed fabric where an intricate design would be lost. I often channel-quilt borders to provide even quilting that won't compete with the central design. Channel quilting is easy to do and doesn't require you to mark the quilt top.

Use thread that matches the fabric, transparent nylon thread, or a neutral color that blends if you'll be quilting over more than one fabric.

1. Attach a walking foot. This special foot will evenly feed the 3 layers of the quilt sandwich through the machine.

2. Use the side of the presser foot as your stitching guide. Align the side of the foot with a seam or previous line of stitching for a uniform channel width.

3. Set the stitch length for 8 to 12 stitches per inch.

4. Pull the bobbin thread to the top of the quilt sandwich and lock the threads. Holding the top thread firmly, take 1 stitch. Tug gently on the top thread and draw the bobbin thread up through the sandwich. Hold both tails firmly and take 4 tiny stitches to anchor the stitching and prevent tangled threads on the back.

5. Begin stitching, keeping your eye on the edge of the presser foot or guide bar.

6. To turn a corner, count the number of stitches required to match the width of the presser foot or channel. Make that many stitches beyond the corner. With the needle down, turn and continue along the next side.

If you're an inexperienced quilter, you may want to practice before starting on your watercolor quilt. Make a simple pieced block or strip-piece a few scraps together, then add a 4" border. Layer your practice piece with batting and backing. Quilt all the seams in-the-ditch, and channel-quilt the border in widths you plan to use on your watercolor quilt.

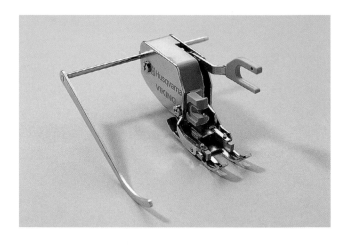

Walking foot with guide bar

When you want a wide channel, insert a guide bar into the left side of the walking foot. Adjust the guide to the desired width and tighten the screw. When you're quilting borders, guiding on the left helps keep the bulk of the quilt sandwich out from underneath the arm of the machine. Use the side that best guides your stitching.

Free-Motion Quilting

Free-motion quilting requires practice but is well worth the effort. Use it to stipple, meander, or follow stencil designs. Use a thread color that matches the quilt top in both the top and bobbin thread. A contrasting bobbin thread can show on the top.

1. Attach a darning foot to allow the quilt sandwich to move freely through the sewing machine. If you don't have a darning foot, use a clear plastic foot such as an open-toe appliqué foot, and remove all the pressure off the foot by releasing the spring on top of the machine. Follow the manufacturer's instructions to adjust your machine settings to "darning."

2. Lower or cover the feed dogs.

3. Pull the bobbin thread to the top of the quilt sandwich and lock the threads. Holding the top thread firmly, take 1 stitch. Tug gently on the top thread and draw the bobbin thread up through the sandwich. Holding both tails firmly, take 4 tiny stitches to anchor the stitching and prevent tangled threads on the back.

4. Start stitching without looking at the needle. Look ahead and behind to see where to go. Stitch at a fairly rapid speed. As with driving, you need to balance your foot speed and hand motion. Find a comfortable speed and develop a rhythm.

Stipple and Meander Quilting

Stipple quilting is a random quilting pattern used to fill open areas and add texture. Use stippling in combination with formal designs, such as feathered wreaths, to make them stand out.

Stippling is like doodling on fabric. Meandering is the same random quilting on a larger scale. The randomness of the stitching allows the background to blend together. There are no crossed lines, no points, and no pattern to attract attention. With a little practice, you'll be able to stipple evenly and beautifully without a marked pattern.

To achieve a random pattern, create rounded knobs like those found on jigsaw puzzles. Keep the width and length of the knobs similar. Match space between stitching lines to the width of the knobs. Pointing knobs up and down is a natural motion similar to regular sewing. Pointing the knobs sideways or diagonally may take some practice, but it adds randomness. Fill in small areas in a swath about 1" to 2" wide. Work side to side: doodle to the left, then drop down below the prior stitching and doodle to the right.

Adding a Hanging Sleeve

To DISPLAY your quilt on a wall, add a hanging sleeve to the back of the quilt. Use a scrap of backing material for a sleeve that blends well. Slip a rod or wood slat through the sleeve to hang the quilt.

Traditional Sleeve

1. Cut an 8½"-wide strip of fabric as long as the width of the quilt. Hem both short ends of the strip.

2. Fold the strip wrong sides together and pin the raw edges to the top of the quilt before you attach the binding. Baste ⅛" from the edge. Sew the binding to the quilt as described on pages 93–95.

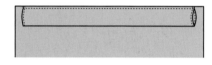

3. Blindstitch the folded edge of the sleeve to the back of your quilt.

Quick-and-Easy Sleeve

1. Before you quilt the final border, add the sleeve. Cut a strip of fabric as wide as the outer border plus 1", and as long as the width of the quilt. Hem both ends of the strip.

2. With right sides together, position the strip on the backing, ½" above the seam joining the outer border to the quilt. Pin the corners securely. Turn the quilt over and stitch in the ditch of the seam joining the outer border to the quilt, catching the sleeve in the stitching. Channel-quilt the top border section only.

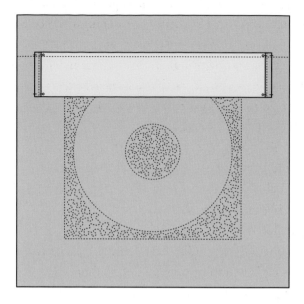

3. After the quilting is complete, remove the pins from the sleeve. Fold the sleeve up, press, and trim away excess. Baste ⅛" from the top edge of the quilt. When you bind the edges, the raw edge will be caught in the stitching. Channel-quilt the side and bottom borders.

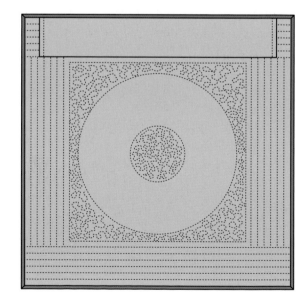

Binding

DOUBLE-FOLD binding adds the durable finishing touch to your quilt. Bind the edges with a fabric that matches the final border or try a contrasting color.

All projects in this book are finished with a straight-grain binding. To cut binding strips, cut across the width of the fabric from selvage to selvage, then join the strips to form a continuous length. A 2½"-wide strip finishes to a ⅜"-wide binding.

To determine the number of binding strips needed, measure the four outer edges of the quilt. Add the measurements, then add 10" to that for a joining allowance. Divide this number by 40", and you'll know how many strips to cut.

Prepare the quilt for binding by removing any safety pins you used for basting and lightly press the hanging sleeve in place. To allow the multiple layers to feed evenly through the machine, use a walking foot when you apply the binding.

1. Cut the number of 2½" strips needed. Lay the first strip with right side up. Lay the second strip, wrong side up, across the first strip at a right angle. Imagine the 2 strips are hands on a clock pointing to 9 o'clock (right side up) and 6 o'clock (wrong side up). Stitch diagonally across the end of the strips.

2. Continue joining the strips to make the length required. Trim the excess and press the seam allowances open.

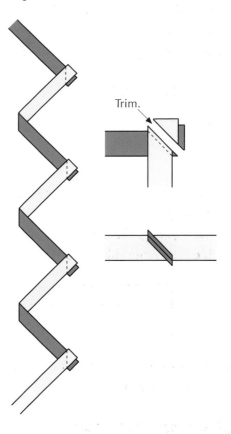

3. Fold the strip in half lengthwise, wrong sides together, and press.

4. Lay the binding along the lower left portion of the quilt—not at a corner—aligning the raw edges. Using a ¼" seam allowance, begin stitching 6" from the end of the strip.

5. Stop stitching ¼" from the corner. With the needle down, pivot and stitch diagonally to the corner.

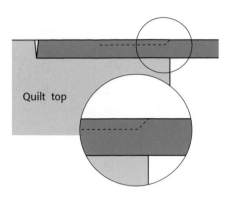

6. Turn the quilt to sew the next side. Fold the binding strip up toward the 12 o'clock position and then down. The fold should line up with the top edge of the quilt, and the raw edges should be even with the side to be stitched. Stitch from the edge to the next corner. Stop ¼" away from the edge, pivot, and stitch diagonally to the corner. Repeat the corner fold. Continue for the remaining corners.

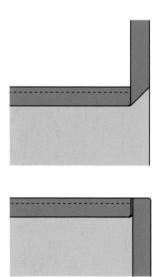

7. After the last corner is stitched, stop. Overlap the ends of the binding. Make a ⅛"-deep clip through all four binding layers. Be careful not to cut the quilt.

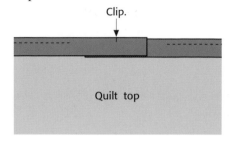

8. Open the folded strips. Lay the ending binding strip, right side up. Lay the beginning binding strip, wrong side up, across the ending strip at a right angle. Imagine the 2 strips are hands on a clock pointing to 9 o'clock (right side up) and 6 o'clock (wrong side up). Use the clips to align the left and top edges of the binding strips as shown. Pin the strips.

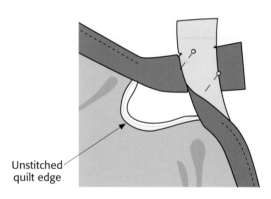

9. Stitch diagonally across the end of the strips. Make certain the joined binding fits, then trim the excess fabric to ¼". Press the seam allowances open.

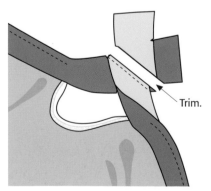

10. Refold the seamed section and align to the quilt edge and complete the stitching.

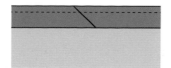

11. Trim the batting and backing even with the raw edges of the binding. Fold the binding to the back over the raw edges of the quilt. The folded edge of the binding should cover the machine stitching. Hand stitch or machine stitch the binding in place, mitering the corners.

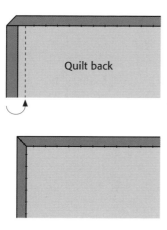

Quilt back

Signing Your Quilt

BE SURE to sign and date your quilt. Labels can be very elaborate or simple. Include the name of the quilt, your name, the city and state where the quilt was completed, the date, the name of the recipient if it is a gift, and any other interesting or important information about the quilt. Include the name of the quilter as well if you have someone else quilt the top for you.

About the Author

DINA PAPPAS is an award-winning quilt-maker, teacher, lecturer, and pattern designer. Her work led to the development of preprinted interfacing for use with watercolor piecing. She is the author of *Quick Watercolor Quilts*. Her quilts have been published by *McCall's Quilting* magazine and seen on the TV show *Simply Quilts*.

Dina began *More Quick Watercolor Quilts* while living in Eagle River, Alaska, with her husband, Jim, and sons Jack and Charley. In Alaska, quilting is not limited to long winter nights; it is a yearlong passion. Endless summer days produce beautiful flowers for inspiration and an occasional snack for the neighborhood moose.

While Dina continued her work on her book, her husband took a job across country. The quilts, fabric, and computer were packed into a trailer, and Dina and her family began a five-thousand-mile drive to their new home, stopping to visit relatives along the way.

"We spent the summer visiting relatives, and my dad told me to make myself at home. I took him up on the offer. He was quite surprised when I unloaded the cutting and sewing tables, sewing machine, and fabric."

The journey ended in Tecumseh, Michigan, where the book was completed and Dina and her family now live. Dina continues to travel around the United States, lecturing, teaching, and encouraging students to give watercolor quilts a try and telling them "Don't fuss." Seeing her students proud of their work and excited about quilting is her reward.